T0244465

光明城
LUMINOCITY

看见我们的未来

骑行上海

关于骑行规划的思考

王卓尔 著

Cycling@Shanghai

A Guide to Cycle Infrastructure

Zhuo'er Wang

同济大学出版社
TONGJI UNIVERSITY PRESS

Contents

目录

Preface

In the autumn of 2018, I encountered the sample of the book on Fengqi Road along the West Lake. It is a small and portable book at first sight, the pictures and texts, which are logically connected with solid evidences interested me a lot. Then I talked to the author with a few cups of tea.

Zhuo'er went to the Netherlands to study for a few years, where she witnessed the well-ordered road system and the charm of cycling in the country. She felt the cycling condition is quite difficult in China and then started working on her book on this subject. Three years of thorough researches and investigations with great patience and persistence have brought up amazing results, where one can find solid resources and argumentation in this book.

I cannot help recalling the days 16 years ago when I entered bicycle industry and started Fahon in south China. The turbulence in business world is like cycling, and I am now in my twilight

序

戊戌之秋，于西湖畔凤起路得此样书一册。初见装帧小巧，轻盈便携，翻之则图文兼备，引证俱全，甚是有趣，遂沏茶相谈。

卓尔赴荷游学数载，睹其街道通达有序，得骑行之趣。归国忽觉骑行不易，故以己之力携同学，询友人，多方考证调研，周转往来中欧，为著书立说。开篇博古通今，面面俱到，内册旁征博引，兼顾中西，议案新奇缜密，图文并茂，可谓尽心竭力。其作业之艰难，非当事者不得同感，其成就之欣喜，仅同行人可以身受。幸小友心恒志坚，三年终得云开月明。

years after struggling for so long. Life is so short in our infinite exploration of the world. Now I would rather enjoy the nature and the pleasure with friends.

I take the encounter with the book and the author as a gift. By the words of this preface, I hope we can always hold such ambition as when we were young.

Min Feng, Founder of Fahon
at West Lake, 2018

忆十六年前，冯某因机缘入自行车行，后辗转南下建立风行。商场沉浮不定，世事繁杂纷纭，有凌云之际，亦有艰难之时，一如骑行。寒来暑往间，忽然已是暮年。但觉人生之须臾不可追，天地之广袤而难穷，不若临长风，饮白露，与宾共适，皆大欢喜。

　　今某遇此书此友，似巧合，亦契机。愿以己度他心，保少年之志，挥笔就序，是以勉励。

风行 DIY 折叠自行车品牌创始人，冯民
2018 年于杭州西湖畔

Foreword

China was once "The Kingdom of Bicycles".[1] Everyone in the country has a personal memory about bicycles. It used to be one of the "three major necessities" for marriage[2,3] and the main means of transportation in the 1970s, but it has been gradually stepped out along with the development of motor vehicles in the 1990s.[4] 20 years later, the drawbacks of the automobile-led urban design gradually emerged. The bicycle, with its low-carbon impact, environmental protection, flexibility and popularity, has come back into our life. Unfortunately, discontinuous cycle ways, obsolete facilities and ill-considered designs made it particularly difficult for people to travel by bicycle.[5]

Since 2015, Office ZHU has been working with the Department of Architecture of Shanghai Jiao Tong University under the theme of Cycling@Shanghai and developed two rounds of research on the bicycle lines in Shanghai. Started with the idea of "cycling", the research group has analyzed the cycling system planning

前言

中国是曾经的"自行车王国"[1]，每个国人或多或少对自行车都有着个人记忆。它曾是结婚"三大件"之一，[2, 3]也是 20 世纪 70 年代主要的代步工具，却随着 90 年代机动车的发展逐渐退出历史舞台[4]。20 年后，以汽车为主导的城市设计弊病逐步显现，自行车以其低碳、环保、灵活和亲民之势再次回归大众视野。然而，不连续的自行车道、陈旧的设施以及有待改善的设计都使得这一出行方式并不如想象的简单。[5]

自 2015 年起，〇筑设计与上海交通大学建筑系合作，以"骑行上海 Cycling@Shanghai"为主题，对上海非机动车道进行了两轮城市研究。我们以"骑行"作为切入

1 Liu Yufeng, The Kingdom of Bicycles. http://www.bilibili.com/video/av4243294/?zw, 1984/2016-04-01.

2 Lai Cunli, Cheng Yanwan, Changes of the Three Major Necessities of Marriage, Reflecting the Major Improvements of People's Life in Zhejiang Province, *Zhejiang Statistics*, 2009 (9).

3 Zhou Kai, Zhang Qi, The Three New Major Necessities of Marriage Challenge Shanghai Families, *The Manager's Daily*, 2007-10-20 (002).

4 Pan Haixiao, The Evolving Cycle Transport Policy in China and Urban Sustainable Development. *Urban Planning Forum*, 2011 (4): 82-86.

5 Jiao Fan, Cycling Journal 1 | It Takes 27 Minutes to Arrive at One Destination by Bicycle and Walk While It Takes 2 Minutes to Make It Illegally. http://www.jfdaily.com/news/detail?id=58313, 2017-07-05/2017-07-10.

1 刘玉峰. 自行车的王国 [OL]. [1984/2016-04-01]. http://www.bilibili.com/video/av4243294/?zw.

2 赖存理，程燕婉. 结婚三大件变迁，折射 60 年浙江民生重大改善 [J]. 浙江统计，2009 (9)：7-9.

3 周凯，张琦. 结婚新三大件考验沪上家庭 [N]. 经理日报，2007-10-20 (002).

4 潘海啸. 中国城市自行车交通政策的演变与可持续发展 [J]. 城市规划学刊，2011 (4)：82-86.

5 焦帆. 骑行日志① | 同一目的地，守法骑行用 27 分钟还得推车步行大半段，违法骑行只要 2 分钟 [N/OL]. [2017-07-05/2017-07-10]. http://www.jfdaily.com/news/detail?id=58313.

of many bike-friendly cities around the world and sorted out current situation of cycling in the downtown area of Puxi district in Shanghai, and further proposed solutions based on this research.

Our research was published on *Urban China* in the end of 2016[6] and attracted the attention of a number of media, including *Jiefang Daily, Southern Weekly, Economic Daily*,[7-9] which interviewed and featured the research as well. To further promote the development of cycling, we want to compile the research into a book, hoping to induce more reactions and studies in Shanghai, a city with more than 20 million people, as well as other cities all over the world.

With the help of 17 young architects that were all born in the 1990s, we managed to complete the research within two years, and the concept of the research was inspired by a group of senior architects. I would like to express my gratitude to Mr. Freek Persyn, Mr. Fan Wenbing, Mr. Don Murphy, who mentored me during my earlier career in architecture and urban research. We would also like to thank the 17 students from the School of Architecture

点，在参考全球自行车友好城市骑行系统规划之后，梳理了上海浦西中心城区的骑行现状，在此基础之上提出方案。

我们的研究自 2016 年底在《城市中国》[6] 发表后，得到了众多媒体的关注，《解放日报》《南方周末》《经济日报》[7-9] 均进行了专访及报道。为了进一步推动慢行系统的发展，我们决定将此项研究编辑成书，希望能抛砖引玉，为这座两千多万人口的城市，乃至更多城市的发展提供一些思路。

在 17 位 90 后年轻建筑师的努力下，该研究得以在两年内完成，而最初的构想也受益于一群先辈建筑师的启发。感谢弗里克·佩森（Freek Persyn）、范文兵和丹·墨菲（Don Murphy）三位导师在建筑及城市研究上给予

6 Office Zhu. Cycling@Shanghai, *Urban China*. 2016-08-24/2017-07-10 http://chuansong.me/n/563077451367, http://chuansong.me/n/710176851667, http://chuansong.me/n/763080751367, http://chuansong.me/n/869634151470, http://chuansong.me/n/960534551170, http://chuansong.me/n/1031330751580.

7 Lei Ceyuan, Way-Finding: Different Possibilities of Cycling in Shanghai. *Jiefang Daily*, 2016-12-19 (09).

8 Tan Chang. NPC&CPPCC Special Feature: How Far Are We with A Kingdom of Bicycles? *Southern Weekend*, http://www.infzm.com/content/123379, 2017-03-10/2017-07-10.

9 Yuan Yong. Where is the Road in-between the Shared Bicycles?. *Economic Daily*, http://www.ce.cn/xwzx/gnsz/gdxw/201705/03/t20170503_22495921.shtml, 2017-05-03/2017-07-10.

6 O 筑设计 . Cycling@Shanghai 骑行上海 [R/OL].
城市中国，[2016-08-24/2017-07-10]. http://chuansong.me/n/563077451367, http://chuansong.me/n/710176851667, http://chuansong.me/n/763080751367, http://chuansong.me/n/869634151470, http://chuansong.me/n/960534551170, http://chuansong.me/n/1031330751580.

7 雷册渊. 寻路：上海骑行的 N 种可能 [N]. 解放日报，2016-12-19 (09).

8 谭畅. 两会特别报道：自行车友好王国有多远？[N/OL]. 南方周末，[2017-03-10/2017-07-10]. http://www.infzm.com/content/123379.

9 袁勇. 共享单车多了，路在哪？[N/OL]. 经济日报，[2017-05-03/2017-07-10]. http://www.ce.cn/xwzx/gnsz/gdxw/201705/03/t20170503_22495921.shtml.

of Jiaotong Univerisity for their great efforts, they are Fu Weijie, Li Jiawen, Shi Jieyu, Wei Yuqi, Xu Yini, Zhou Shiyao, Zhang Tianyun, Chen Zhushen, Huang Tao, Liu Mengdi, Jin Chi, Jin Mengyi, Shou Chengbin, Tang Huilian, Yin Zheng, Zhang Yuyuan and Zhu Yichen. At last, on behalf of the research team, I would like to express my gratitude to studio Haller Brun, the designers of this book, as well as graphic designer Wu Long for his kind help. It is with all your great support that we managed to publish the results of our research.

Zhuo'er Wang
October 2018

的引导；也感谢付炜杰、李佳雯、施捷雨、魏宇琦、徐旖旎、周诗耀、张天韵、陈柱燊、黄涛、刘梦迪、金池、金梦怡、寿成彬、唐慧莲、殷正、张愉源、朱奕臣这 17 位交大建筑系学生的付出。最后，我谨代表研究团队感谢设计本书的哈勒·布朗工作室（Studio Haller Brun），以及平面设计师吴龙的协助，在他们的设计及帮助下，研究结果得以面世。

王卓尔

2018 年 10 月

概述｜自行车发展史

Overview:
Development of the Bicycle

In the 1980s, China was listed in the top in the world for the number of bicycle ownership. Shanghai used to be the largest bicycle production base at that time, and cycling was one of the main means of commuting in Shanghai. However, with the accelerating expansion of the city and the rapid growth of mechanization in the 1990s, the streets were gradually taken by motor vehicles, and the cycling conditions were getting worse. Statistics showed that the cycling travel ratio was decreased by 60% from 1995 to 2009 in Shanghai.[1]

There are many domestic researches based upon this transformation as well as the urban issues it evoked, among which there is a portion that refers to cases in foreign countries, yet most researches are mainly resulted in texts and focus on one particular aspect, and with few chance we will be able to find studies that are more systemic or address to a particular city. To make a remedy, our team adopted a research-based design method and started with the history of bicycle. Based on the downtown area of Puxi, we sorted out the existing cycling condition of Shanghai

20世纪80年代，中国自行车拥有量居世界前列。在当时最大的自行车生产基地——上海，骑行一度是市民主要的出行方式。然而，随着90年代城市的迅速扩张与城市机动化水平的快速提高，以机动车为主导的路权分配倾向逐步显现，骑行环境日趋恶化。数据表明，自1995年至2009年，上海自行车出行比率下降了60%。[1]

对于这一转变以及随之而来的城市问题，国内相似的研究和对国外案例的引介并不少见。然而，就现有资料来看，多数成果依然以文字为主且仅涵盖某一方面，而少有系统性的研究，或对某一城市提出具体愿景。为了补足这一缺失，我们采取了研究式设计方法，从自行车发展历史入手，以浦西中心城区为主要研究对象，通过资料搜集和绘图的方式，初步理清了上海当下的骑行

1   汤暘，刘魏巍，潘海啸. 城市政策对上海的自行车发展及骑行的影响 [DB/OL]. [2014-09-13/2017-07-10]. http://cpfd.cnki.com.cn/Article/CPFDTOTAL-ZHCG201409005003.htm.

1   Tang Yang, Liu Weiwei, Pan Haixiao. The Influence of Municipal Policy on the Development of Bicycle and Cycling in Shanghai. http://cpfd.cnki.com.cn/Article/CPFDTOTAL-ZHCG201409005003.htm, 2014-09-13/2017-07-10.

through data collection and mapping, and evaluate the streets in downtown area through onsite investigation. After case study over the bike-friendly cities worldwide, the team carried out an overall conception of the future cycling system in the central areas and designed on pilot sites and roads.

状况，并通过实地考察对市区的道路进行评分。在参考了全球自行车友好城市案例、分析了上海现有空间特点之后，我们对中心城区未来的骑行系统展开整体构想，并抽取部分样本基地及路段进行设计。

20世纪80年代的中国骑行者
Chinese cyclists in 1980s

The History and Status of Bicycles: Beyond Commuter Tools

As a mechanical installation, the bike was invented two hundred years ago. It was more than a tool of commuting as it was defined today. It was first introduced as a new technology, and then become a sport. In peace times, it serves civilians, and was turned into an armament during the war. In recent years, bicycles have become a financing tool in the context of Internet technology. In order to expand people's understanding of bicycles and cycling, our team drew a timeline (see "History of the Bicycle Development" on the insert sheet). On top it is the development of bicycles throughout the world, and domestic development below. In addition, the study also extracted some important events to help readers understand the future trends and the current position.

自行车的历史及现况：超越通勤工具

作为一种机械装置，自行车自发明以来已有两百多年历史。尽管就今天而言，自行车多被认为是一种通勤工具，然而在过去，其价值远不止于此。最初，它是一种新科技；随后，被引入比赛成为体育用品。和平时代，它服务于平民；战争期间，它成为军事装备之一；近几年，在互联网技术的配合下，自行车又成为了融资工具。为了拓展对自行车及骑行的认知，在搜集了相关历史资料后，我们制作了一张"自行车发展史"的时间表（见插页图表）。时间轴上方为自行车全球发展历程，而下方则为国内发展历程。有关自行车本身的史料、政策、影像被纪录于此。此外，研究也摘录了一些重要事件，以帮助读者了解其当时所处的地位以及之后的发展趋势。

From a Mechanical Device and Daily Necessity
to a War Tool – Bicycles Worldwide

German Baron Karl von Drais is commonly known as the inventor of bicycles. He began to make cart with wooden wheels in 1818, and then added a handlebar to control and change the direction, but it still needs to be ridden by feet and was called "pony".[2] In 1886, British mechanical engineer Starley designed a new type of bicycle by installing the front fork and brake, which has made the front wheel and back wheel into the same size to keep the balance, and rubber wheels were used for the first time. The form of the bicycle designed by Starley is almost the same as the present type.[3] The first cycle lane in the world was built by the Dutch in 1890.[4] In late 1890 when the first bicycle was invented almost 100 years ago, bicycling has become more convenient and secure with the development of rotating chains and the pneumatic tire, marking a significant growth in bike industry.[5] In 1896, road cycling was first introduced to the Summer Olympic Games.[6] During World War I, the British, American, Italian and German armies organized their own bicycle troops.[7] Similar troops are also used in WWII. However, although the total number of bicycles was increasing, the bicycle industry stops growing after WWII. With the development of vehicle in the

从机械装置，日用品，到战争工具：自行车在全球

德国男爵冯·德莱斯被公认为自行车的发明人，1818年他开始制作木轮车。他在前轮上加了一个控制方向的车把，以改变前进的方向，骑车人要用两只脚蹬地使车前行，这种木轮车被称为"木马"[2]。1886年，英国的机械工程师斯塔利设计出新的自行车样式。他给自行车装上前叉和车闸，使前后轮大小相同以保持平衡，并首次使用了橡胶车轮。这款自行车车型与今天自行车的样子已基本一致[3]。随着自行车产业的发展，1890年世界上第一条自行车专用道出现，其建造者为荷兰人[4]。而在1890年中后期，第一辆自行车诞生近百年后，随着链传动自行车以及充气胎的发明，骑行变得更为安全、舒适，自行车行业终于迎来了发展风潮[5]。之后，公路自行车比赛甚至被纳入1896年的夏季奥运会[6]。而自行车被大量应用于战争则是在第一次世界大战期间，英、美、意、德军队均组建

2　李峰. 国外自行车交通发展简史[J]. 交通与运输，1995 (04)：42-43.

3　John Kemp Starley [DB/OL]. [2011-01-04/2017-07-10]. https://en.wikipedia.org/wiki/John_Kemp_Starley.

4　顾尚华. 各国自行车交通的发展[J]. 交通与运输，2009 (01)：28-30.

5　Bike boom. [DB/OL]. [2017-06-10/2017-07-11]. https://en.wikipedia.org/wiki/Bike_boom.

6　Cycling at the summer Olympics. [DB/OL]. [2017-06-21/2017-07-11] https://en.wikipedia.org/wiki/Cycling_at_the_Summer_Olympics.

2　Li Feng, A Brief History of Bicycle Transportation in Foreign Countries. *Traffic & Transportation*, 1995 (04): 42-43.

3　John Kemp Starley, Wikipedia, https://en.wikipedia.org/wiki/John_Kemp_Starley, 2011-01-04/2017-07-10.

4　Gu Shanghua. The Development of Bicycle Transportation in Different Countries. *Traffic & Transportation*. 2009 (01): 28-30 2013-12-07/2017-07-11.

5　Bike boom. Wikipedia, https://en.wikipedia.org/wiki/Bike_boom, 2017-06-10/2017-07-11.

6　Cycling at the summer Olympics. Wikipedia, https://en.wikipedia.org/wiki/Cycling_at_the_Summer_Olympics, 2017-06-21/2017-07-11.

7　Bicycle infantry. Wikipedia, https://en.wikipedia.org/wiki/Bicycle_infantry, 2017-05-29/2017-07-11.

1950s, the cycling condition is getting worse. In 1971, 3,000 cyclists died in Netherland because of vehicles. 450 of whom were children under 14. This event raised the movement of "Stop the Children Murder" to improve riding safety. Soon after, the country carried out "Car-Free Sunday" when motor vehicles were forbidden in the downtown area. During the same period in 1973, the fourth Arab-Israeli War triggered the first oil crisis, which led the Western world to re-examine the risk of energy in the automotive industry and the value of non-motor vehicles. Cycling regained to people's attention.[8-10] In 1975, the Dutch government began to build safe and independent cycle lanes in Tilburg and the Hague, and then the ratio of cycling in Tilburg increased by 70%.[11] In 1990, the German Railway launched a project that allows people to bring bicycles on the rail train.[12] Nowadays, the bicycle is not only a tool of transportation. More and more different types of bicycles have started to become part of our lives.

了自己的自行车部队[7]。类似的做法被沿用到第二次世界大战期间。虽然自行车总体数量上升，但是战后自行车的发展却陷入了低谷。随着20世纪50年代私人汽车的风靡，骑行环境逐步恶化。1971年，荷兰有3 000人因机动车丧生，其中450名是儿童，为此荷兰掀起了"停止谋杀儿童"的运动，以呼吁大众重视骑行安全。随后，"无车周日"开始实行，市中心开始禁行机动车。同一时期的1973年，第四次中东战争引发了第一次石油危机，西方开始重新审视汽车工业所带来的能源风险和非机动车的价值，骑行被提倡，自行车逐步复兴[8-10]。1975年，荷兰政府开始建设独立的自行车道，并在蒂尔堡和海牙投入建造，之后蒂尔堡骑行出行率增加了70%[11]。德国也随即在1990年推出"自行车搭乘轨道列车"项目，允许人们携带自行车搭乘城市公共短途轨道列车。与此同时，自行车产品本身也在持续发展，至21世纪，自行车已不仅仅是一种代步工具，不同类型的自行车开始进入人们的生活。

8　Mark Wagenbuur. Amsterdam children fighting cars in 1972. *Bicycle Dutch*, https://bicycledutch.wordpress.com/2013/12/12/amsterdam-children-fighting-cars-in-1972/, 013-12-01/2017-07-11.

9　Mark Wagenbuur. Car Free Sundays, a 40 year anniversary. *Bicycle Dutch*, https://bicycledutch.wordpress.com/2013/12/01/car-free-sundays-a-40-year-anniversary/, 2013-12-01/2017-07-11.

10　Anna Holligan. *Why is cycling so popular in the Netherlands?* BBC, http://www.bbc.com/news/magazine-23587916/, 2013-08-08/2017-07-11.

11　Mark Wagenbuur. How the Dutch got their cycling infrastructure. *Bicycle Dutch*, https://bicycledutch.wordpress.com/2011/10/20/how-the-dutch-got-their-cycling-infrastructure/, 2011-10-20/2017-07-11.

7　Bicycle infantry. [DB/OL]. [2017-05-29/2017-07-11]. https://en.wikipedia.org/wiki/Bicycle_infantry.

8　Mark Wagenbuur. Amsterdam children fighting cars in 1972 [R/OL]. Bicycle Dutch, [2013-12-01/2017-07-11] https://bicycledutch.wordpress.com/2013/12/12/amsterdam-children-fighting-cars-in-1972/.

9　Mark Wagenbuur. Car Free Sundays, a 40 year anniversary [R/OL]. Bicycle Dutch, [2013-12-01/2017-07-11] https://bicycledutch.wordpress.com/2013/12/01/car-free-sundays-a-40-year-anniversary/.

10　Anna Holligan. Why is cycling so popular in the Netherlands? [R/OL]. BBC, [2013-08-08/2017-07-11] http://www.bbc.com/news/magazine-23587916t.

11　Mark Wagenbuur. How the Dutch got their cycling infrastructure [R/OL]. Bicycle Dutch, [2011-10-20/2017-07-11] https://bicycledutch.wordpress.com/2011/10/20/how-the-dutch-got-their-cycling-infrastructure/.

From an Imported Good, One of the "Three Pieces"
to a Financing Tool – Bicycles in China

Compared with the development in the western world, the bicycle industry in China is a bit delayed. In China, the term "Bicycle" first appeared in 1866 when the Qing government sent the first overseas delegation. The 19-year-old delegate Zhang Deyi mentioned the word "zixingche" in his travel journal, which he explained as a vehicle that could move under man's power.[12] The first recorded proof of bicycle introduced into China is an article published by *The Chinese Shipping List & Advertiser* on Nov. 24th, 1868, saying that "I saw several bicycles in Shanghai".[13] In China, the first peak of bicycle development appeared in 1941. It was the moment of the Anti-Japanese War when the gasoline supply is severely limited in Shanghai, and the number of cars shrunk dramatically. Even the trams were largely stopped working. In addition to rickshaws, the transportation in Shanghai was mainly undertaken by bicycles and tricycles. In the following 20 years, local bicycle brands started to boom in China, such as Shanghai Forever in 1940, Tianjin Pigeon in 1950 and Shanghai Phoenix in 1958. In the 1960s and 1970s, the bicycle was known as one of "the three must-have items for marriage" in China, which were important necessities

从舶来品，三大件，到融资工具：自行车在中国

与国外自行车发展相比，中国自行车的起步略晚。在中国，"自行车"一词最早出现在1866年。1866年清廷派出了第一个出洋考察团，19岁少年张德彝参加考察，他在游记里提到"自行车"这一名词[12]，意为靠个人自己的力量使其行走的车子。而自行车传入中国的最早证据见于1868年11月24日《上海新报》的一篇文章："兹见上海地方有自行车几辆"[13]。国内的第一个自行车高峰出现在1941年，抗日战争爆发后，上海汽油供给受到严重限制，汽车数量大幅缩水，电车也多半停止运营。承担上海交通任务的除人力车外，几乎全部为自行车和由其改装的三轮车。在随后的20年内，国产自行车品牌开始涌现，如1940年的上海永久、1950年的天津飞鸽、1958年的上海凤凰。到了20世纪六七十年代，自行车被誉为"结婚三大件"之一，它是女孩子当时找婆家的首要物质

12 张德彝. 欧美环游记[M/OL]. [2015-06-11/
    2017-07-12]. https://drive.google.com/file/d/
    0B-KzoocHj_Qdanl2MjBVUnJWSGs/view.
13 郑薛飞腾. 自行车归来：它在中国经历了怎样
    的百年发展[N/OL]. 澎湃新闻，[2017-04-01/
    2017-07-12]. http://www.thepaper.cn/
    newsDetail_forward_1650632.

12 Zhang Deyi. Traveling around Europe. https://drive.
    google.com/file/d/0B-KzoocHj_Qdanl2MjBVUnJWSGs/
    view, 2015-06-11/ 2017-07-12.
13 Zheng Xuefeiteng. The Return of Bicycle: A Hundred Years
    of Development of Bicycle in China. The Paper,
    http://www.thepaper.cn/newsDetail_forward_1650632,
    2017-04-01/ 2017-07-12.

for people to get married. In the 1980s, bicycle industry kept growing, and China was called the "Kingdom of Bicycles".[14] The year 1994 is the important turning point in China's bicycle history, because the State Council published the first automotive industry policy which openly declared that the government encouraged the individual to purchase cars. Since then, the idea of forbidding private automobile was overturned.[15] At the same time, bicycle began to gradually retreat from people's life in Chinese metropolises. In 2002, it was clearly defined that the absolute number of bicycles would be reduced by 25% between 2000 and 2005 in the white paper of *Urban and Public Transportation in Shanghai*.[16] In the 2008 Olympic Games, Beijing launched the bicycle rent service. However, the market continued to shrink after the event. Beijing Bicycle Rental Co, retained only 12 of the 200 branches. In 2012, there were only a few hundred bicycles available.[17] In 2013, the city slow traffic system was brought up again. In the new white paper of *Development Strategy of the Urban and Public Transportation in Shanghai*, the government proposed to optimize the cycle route network and to build a continuous cycling system in Shanghai.[18] By the end of 2016, with the development of Internet technology, the sharing bicycle system had emerged in the city again; within half a year, there had been dozens of brands in the market because of the influx of venture capital.

条件。20世纪80年代期间，国内自行车产业持续发展，中国被称为"自行车王国"[14]。1994年是中国自行车发展史上一个重要转折点，国务院公布了第一个《汽车工业产业政策》，公开表示国家鼓励个人购买汽车[15]。也正是从那时开始，在中国的大城市中，自行车开始逐渐淡出人们的生活。2002年，《上海市城市交通白皮书》中甚至明确提出计划在2000至2005年间将自行车绝对数量减少25%[16]。2008年奥运会期间，北京曾一度兴建自行车租赁服务设施。然而奥运会后，北京自行车租赁市场萎缩，贝科蓝图公司只保留了当年200个联网点中的12个，2012年仅几百辆自行车仍用于出租[17]。2013年，政策又开始向慢行系统倾斜，新一轮《上海市交通发展白皮书》提出要完善自行车出行路网，以构建系统、连续的骑行网络为目标[18]。2016年底，结合互联网技术，扫码即骑的共享单车进入各大城市。随着资本的涌入，短短半年内几十个品牌蜂拥而出。

14　Xu Tao. Bicycle and Modern China (1868–1949). Shanghai: East China Normal University, 2012: 76-77.
15　Analyst of People's Daily. Major Initiatives to Promote Healthy Development in Automobile Industry. People's Daily, 2004-06-02 (06).
16　Pan Haixiao. The Evolvement and Sustainable Development of Bicycle Transportation Policies in Urban China. Urban Planning Forum, 2011 (4) 82-86.
17　Feng Su. Who Moved China's Bicycle. Netease News, http://news.163.com/photoview/3R710001/11177.html#p=6I76BCCN3R710001, 2012-08-03/2017-07-12.
18　Editorial Office of White Paper of Development Strategy of the Urban and Public Transportation in Shanghai. White Paper of Development Strategy of the Urban and Public Transportation in Shanghai, http://sh.eastday.com/bps.pdf, 2013-08-23/2017-07-12.

14　徐涛. 自行车与近代中国（1868–1949年）[D]. 上海: 华东师范大学, 2012: 76-77.
15　人民日报评论员. 人民日报: 汽车产业健康发展的重大举措[N]. 人民日报, 2004-06-02(06).
16　潘海啸. 中国城市自行车交通政策的演变与可持续发展[J]. 城市规划学刊, 2011(4): 82-86.
17　冯骦. 谁动了中国的自行车[N]. 网易新闻, [2012-08-03/2017-07-12]. http://news.163.com/photoview/3R710001/11177.html#p=6I76BCCN3R710001.
18　《上海市交通发展白皮书》编制领导小组办公室. 上海市交通发展白皮书[EB/OL]. [2013-08-23/2017-07-12]. http://sh.eastday.com/bps.pdf.

History of the Bicycle Development

The timeline shows the development of the bicycle industry since 1790. Influential bicycle brands, events and media works related to cycling are recorded here. The above part is the history from developed country, while the below part is the one from China. Through this timeline, the peak and trough of bicycle development are easy to see, it also helps us to understand the status quo of China's bicycle industry.

自行车发展史

此图展示了自1790年起的自行车工业发展历史，记录了具有时代影响力的自行车品牌与骑行相关事件，以及影视作品。时间轴上方为国外自行车发展历程，下方则是中国发展历程。据此可见自行车发展的高峰与低谷期，以及中国自行车产业的发展现况。

时间表缩略图（详见插页图表）
Thumbnail of the Timeline (see larger version on the insert sheet)

From Development and Declination to Revival – Cycling in Shanghai

The development of cycling in Shanghai has experienced four stages since reform and opening up.

The first stage is from the beginning of the 1980s to 1995 when Shanghai experienced a new round of urban expansion. Because the public transportation service was lagged behind, the middle and long-distance travel that should have been supported by public transportation vehicles were in fact supported by bicycles and motorcycles. At this stage, the use of bicycles was increasing rapidly from 13% in 1981 to 32.8% in 1995.

The second stage is from 1995 to 2005, *The Automotive Industry Policy* openly declared that the government encouraged the individual to purchase automobiles, meanwhile Shanghai started the construction of subway. At this stage, some cyclists turned to use other means of transportation, and the ratio of cycling declined rapidly (see "Status of Trip Mode Changes in Shanghai", p. 44).

The third stage is from 2005 to 2016. In this period, urban expansion kept accelerating, and the growth of cars is prominent. In 2004, China has launched the project of changing non-motor lanes into motor vehicle lanes, which has not only degraded the rights of the cyclists, but also

从发展，衰落，到复兴：骑行在上海

自改革开放以来，上海自行车交通的发展主要经历了四个阶段。

第一阶段：从20世纪80年代初到90年代初，上海开始新一轮城市化进程。由于公共交通服务的滞后，本应由公共交通承担的中距离、甚至长距离出行在实际城市生活中是由自行车和助动车承担的。在这一阶段，自行车出行比例不断增长，从1981年市区的13%增长到1995年的32.8%。

第二阶段：从1995年至2005年，由于《汽车工业产业政策》公开表示"国家鼓励个人购买汽车"，同时，上海轨道交通开始建设，这一时期部分骑行人群转向其他出行方式，自行车出行比例逐年下降（见"上海市历年出行方式结构变化统计"，P44）。

第三阶段：从2005年至2016年，随着机动车数量增多，以及2004年开始的"非改机"工程正式实施，骑行者的基本路权受

blocked the cycling route network, especially in the central areas in the city.

The fourth stage started from 2016 when the bicycle sharing services appeared. According to the date from Shanghai Consumer Council in 2017, more than 30 companies provided bicycle sharing business, and there were around 0.45 million sharing bicycles in Shanghai. When solving the problems on the "last mile" trip, the sharing bicycles also brings new challenges to cycle path and parking.

Although the cycling spaces are shrinking, and the cycle infrastructure is far from sufficiency, cycling in Shanghai still has great potential from the perspective of energy safety,[19] finance,[20] urban character and geography (see "Future Tendency Analysis: Energy Crisis", p. 45).[21] Also, since slow traffic system planning has become more and more important after the oil crisis, with the proposing of *Shanghai 2040, Shanghai Street Design Guideline*, cycling will revive in the coming future in Shanghai.

到挤压，原本连续的骑行网络也被打断。这一问题在中心城区尤为明显。

第四阶段：从2016年底共享单车涌现开始。2017年初上海市消保委的数据显示，共有超过30家企业开展共享单车业务，其中无桩共享单车投放总量达45万辆。共享单车在解决"最后一公里"出行问题的同时，也给现有的骑行道路规划、停车设施带来新的挑战。

尽管就目前骑行现况来看，非机动车路权被挤压、设施缺乏是事实，但基于能源安全[19]、经济性[20]、城区特点以及地形[21]，在上海，骑行拥有巨大的潜力及优势（见"未来趋势分析"，P45）。

此外，随着石油危机之后慢行系统在规划领域逐渐受到重视，以及近几年《上海2040》《上海市街道设计导则》的相继编制与公示，我们可以预见，未来在上海，骑行将迎来复兴。

19 Chen Mo. New Thoughts on China's Energy Security. West Asia and Africa, http://qk.cass.cn/xyfz/qkml/2012year/6/201212/P020131222027783016413.pdf, 2012-04/2017-07-12.

20 Ying Shi. What Should We Do When the Price of Car Plate is over RMB90,000? Shanghai Securities News, 2013-03-24 (004).

21 Sitting in the middle and lower plain of Changjiang River, Shanghai is a city where different functions are highly mixed in its central district. Shanghai Planning and Land Resource Administration Bureau. Urban Planning Map in Central Shanghai, http://www.shgtj.gov.cn/xxgk/ghjh/201503/W020160125402251538384.jpg, 2016-01-25/2017-7-12.

19 陈沫. 中国能源安全新思考[J]. 西亚非洲, [2012-04/2017-07-12] http://qk.cass.cn/xyfz/qkml/2012year/6/201212/P0201312202 77830165413.pdf.

20 应时. 上海私车牌照价格突破9万元后该怎么办？. 上海证券报, 2013-03-25(004).

21 上海位于长江中下游平原，地势平坦，中心城区内功能高度混合，参考上海市规划及国土资源管理局. 上海市中心城总体规划图[EB/OL]. [2016-01-25/2017-7-12] http://www.shgtj.gov.cn/xxgk/ghjh/201503/W020160125402251538384.jpg.

自行车道被公共汽车占用，2012，北京
Cycle lane occupied by a bus, 2012, Bejing

上海市历年出行方式结构变化统计
Status of Trip Mode Changes in Shanghai

年份 Year	范围 Range	出行方式结构（%） Trip mode percentage (%)					
		轨道 Rail	公交 Bus	出租 Taxi	个体机动 Personal motor vehicle	非机动 Non-motor vehicle	步行 Walk
1981	市区 Downtown	0	28	0	1	13	58
1986	市区 Downtown	0	35	0	3	26	37
1995	中心城区 Central city	0.9	21.2	4	6	32.8	35
	全市 The whole city	0.6	16.4	3	7.9	41.7	30.4
2005	中心城区 Central city	4.8	19.9	8.6	15.3	23.2	28.2
	全市 The whole city	3.1	14.6	6.5	17.6	29.3	28.8
2007	中心城区 Central city	5.6	18.7	8.2	16.6	22.5	28.4
	全市 The whole city	3.6	13.3	6.1	19.7	28.9	28.4
2009	中心城区 Central city	8.7	17.1	8.8	19.5	19.5	26.5
	全市 The whole city	5.7	12.9	6.6	20	28.7	26.2

资料来源：汤諹，刘薇薇，潘海啸．城市政策对上海非自行车发展及骑行的影响 [DB/OL]．[2014/2017-7-14] http://cpfd.cnki.com.cn/Article/CPFDTOTAL-ZHCG201409005003.htm
Source: Tang Yang, Liu Weiwei, Pan Haixiao. The influence of Municipal Policy on the Development of Bicycle and Cycling in Shanghai [DB/OL]. http://cpfd.cnki.com.cn/

未来趋势分析：能源危机
Future Tendency Analysis: Energy Crisis

中国的产油量与耗油量
Oil production and consumption of China (1993 – 2015)

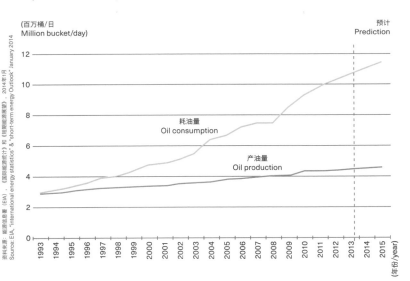

购车成本（元）
Costs of owning a car (CNY)

	2004	2015	涨幅 Amount of increase
一箱油 One box of oil	140	400	185%
牌照 License plate	30 000	80 000	166%
学车费用 Cost of learning driving	3 000	10 000	233%

未来趋势分析：自行车vs汽车
Future Tendency Analysis: Bicycle versus Automobile

生活成本
Living costs

月/Month

收入/Income
¥7 400

餐食/Meal
–¥1 500

住宿/Accomodation
–¥3 000

余额/Balance
¥2 900

购车成本
Car costs

购自行车成本
Bicycle costs

轿车/Car
¥100 000

牌照/Licence plate
¥80 000

自行车/Bycicle
¥2 400

投入/Asset cost
¥180 000

投入/Asset cost
¥2 400

汽车、自行车维护费用比对
Car and bike maintenance costs comparison

月/month

余额/Balance
¥2 900

月/month

余额/Balance
¥2 900

汽油/Petrol
– ¥800

—

停车/Parking
– ¥400

停车/Parking
– ¥60

维修/Repairs
– ¥350

维修/Repairs
– ¥30

养护/Maintenance
– ¥450

—

剩余/Savings
¥900

剩余/Savings
¥2 810

注：以上数据由研究团队从于2014年问卷调查所得。
Source: The above data was obtained from the 2014 survey by the research team.

0 磅/pounds

260 磅/pounds

451 磅/pounds

859 磅/pounds

1 235 磅/pounds

1 837 磅/pounds

汽车、自行车停车位比对
Parking spaces comparison

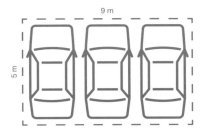

3 辆车
3 cars

=

20 辆自行车
20 bicycles

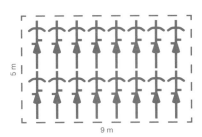

现状研究｜上海浦西中心城区
骑行现状

Current Situation:
Shanghai Puxi Downtown
Cycling Condition

How is the cycling condition in the most populous downtown area of Puxi? What's its strengths and potential compared with worldwide bicycle friendly cities? Which areas have better cycling conditions and which ones are worse? The team collected data and analyzed this.

上海人口最密集的浦西中心城区现有骑行状况如何？与全球自行车友好城市相比，其优势和潜力到底在哪里？哪些区域骑行环境不错，哪些较差？我们对此予以了数据采集及分析。

Research Scope

We set the scope of our study in the seven downtown districts which share the densest population in Shanghai: Huangpu District, Jing'an District, Xuhui District, Changning District, Putuo District, Hongkou District and Yangpu District. The total area is 290 km² with the population of 6.9 million, and the density of population is 24,000 people per km².[1] The main characteristics of these areas are high population dinsity, multiple functions and flat terrain, which also provide great convenience for cycling. As the earliest city centers, they embrace a major part of citizens commuting via cycling. In order to explore the feasibility of establishing independent cycling system in Shanghai, we make a scale comparison between Shanghai and other bicycle-friendly cities around the world (see "City Scale Comparison", pp. 60 – 63).

At this stage, we referred to the top 20 cycling-friendly cities listed in 2015 Copenhagenize Index as well as mentioned in *Cycle Infrastructure*,[2] and picked out 16 well-developed cities with unique characteristics for scale comparison. The biggest city is Berlin (891.85 km²), and the smallest is Nantes (65.19 km²). Shanghai is between Berlin and Nantes

研究范围

我们将研究范围设定在上海人口最为集中的市中心七个区：黄浦区、静安区、徐汇区、长宁区、普陀区、虹口区、杨浦区。其总面积约为 290 km²，人口为 699 万人，人口密度为 2.4 万人 /km²。[1] 该区域人口密度高，功能混合，地势平坦，有利于骑行。作为最早的中心城区，居住于此的大部分本地市民都曾以骑行来通勤。为了探究在上海这座城市建立何种骑行系统更具有可实施性，我们又将上海与国外自行车友好城市进行了规模比对。（见"城市规模对比"，P60–P63）

在评估了"2015 哥本哈根指数"评选出来的世界前 20 个自行车友好城市，以及《骑行设施》[2] 一书中提及的自行车友好城市后，我们选择了 16 个城市，本书收录了最具代表性的 7 个城市作为案例分析。其中柏林面积最大，为 891.85 km²，南特的面积最小，

1　Shanghai. [DB/OL]. [2017-4-12/2017-07-12] https://en.wikipedia.org/wiki/Shanghai.

2　Stefan Bendinks, Aglaee Degros. Cycle Infrastructure[M]. Rotterdam: Nai010, 2013: 24-25, 32-107.

1　Shanghai. https://en.wikipedia.org/wiki/Shanghai. 2017-4-12/2017-07-12.

2　Stefan Bendinks, Aglaee Degros. Cycle Infrastructure. Rotterdam: Nai010, 2013: 24-25, 32-107.

in terms of scale. Therefore, we believe that the city centers of Shanghai own great potential of becoming a bicycle-friendly, and the cycling system here is very likely to be extended to the outer areas in the future.

为 65.19 km²，而上海则介于两者之间。因此，就城市规模而言，我们认为上海中心城区具有发展自行车友好城市的骑行系统的潜力，并且存在未来骑行系统向外延伸的可行性。

城市规模对比
City Scale Comparison

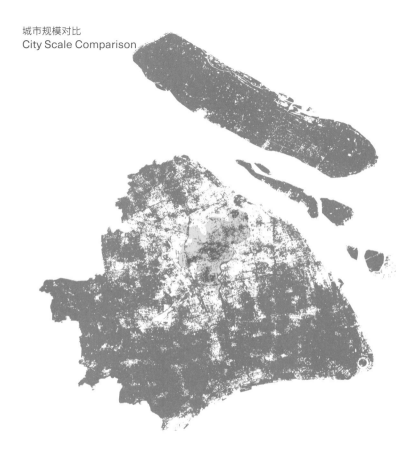

上海 Shanghai

面积 Area: 6 340.50 km²
人口 Population: 24 151 500 人 people
人口密度 Population density: 3 800 人 people / km²

中心城区 City Center

面积 Area: 288.90 km²
人口 Population: 6 203 976 人 people
人口密度 Population density: 21 474 人 people / km²

柏林 Berlin
面积 Area: 891.85 km²
人口 Population: 3 562 166 人 people
人口密度 Population density: 4 000 人 people/km²

维也纳 Vienna
面积 Area: 414.65 km²
人口 Population: 1 794 770 人 people
人口密度 Population density: 4 002.2 人 people/km²

蒙特利尔 Montreal
面积 Area: 365.10 km²
人口 Population: 1 649 519 人 people
人口密度 Population density: 4 517.6 人 people/km²

鹿特丹 Rotterdam
面积 Area: 325.79 km²
人口 Population: 619 679 人 people
人口密度 Population density: 2 969 人 people/km²

阿姆斯特丹 Amsterdam
面积 Area: 219.32 km²
人口 Population: 813 562 人 people
人口密度 Population density: 4 906 人 people/km²

安特卫普 Antwerp
面积 Area: 204.51 km²
人口 Population: 502 604 人 people
人口密度 Population density: 2 500 人 people/km²

现状研究

61

乌珀塔尔 Wuppertal
面积 Area: 168.41 km²
人口 Population: 343 468 人 people
人口密度 Population density: 2 000 人 people/km²

明尼阿波利斯 Minneapoli
面积 Area: 151.30 km²
人口 Population: 407 207 人 people
人口密度 Population density: 2 863 人 people/km²

都柏林 Dublin
面积 Area: 114.99 km²
人口 Population: 527 612 人 people
人口密度 Population density: 4 566 人 people/km²

温哥华 Vancouver
面积 Area: 114.97 km²
人口 Population: 603 502 人 people
人口密度 Population density: 5 249 人 people/km²

巴黎 Paris
面积 Area: 105.40 km²
人口 Population: 2 273 305 人 people
人口密度 Population density: 22 000 人 people/km²

巴塞罗那 Barcelona
面积 Area: 101.40 km²
人口 Population: 1 604 555 人 people
人口密度 Population density: 16 000 人 people/km²

里斯本 Lisbon
面积 Area: 100.05 km²
人口 Population: 552 700 人 people
人口密度 Population density: 6 458 人 people/km²

乌得勒支 Utrecht
面积 Area: 99.32 km²
人口 Population: 330 772 人 people
人口密度 Population density: 3 507 人 people/km²

哥本哈根 Copenhagen
面积 Area: 86.20 km²
人口 Population: 579 510 人 people
人口密度 Population density: 6 700 人 people/km²

南特 Nantes
面积 Area: 65.19 km²
人口 Population: 284 970 人 people
人口密度 Population density: 4 400 人 people/km²

Cycling Today

Shanghai's existing bicycle lanes are built along the road system. In the drawing "Shanghai Existing Bicycle Lanes", p. 68, the strips from dark blue to light gray are in sequence high-speed road, the main road, the secondary road and branch road. Red dotted line, as planned by the Shanghai government, is the non-bicycle lane. The red strip is the one-way cycling lane. From the map, you will find out that the non-cycling roads are mainly located inside the inner ring road of Shanghai.[3]

Before making a proposal, we would like to know how the cyclists value the current cycling environment of Shanghai's city center. This map shows the results studied by Professor Zhu Wei from Urban Planning and Design Institute of Tongji University on the cycling environment. The deeper the color goes, the lower the condition for cycling is. The map shows whether it is the main road, the secondary road, or the branch road, there are always sections with poor cycling experience all over the central areas, particularly in Huangpu District and Hongkou District (see "Cycling Environment Evaluation", p. 69).[4]

To further understand the relationship between cycling environment and road condition,[5] our team made a chart to evaluate cycling experience,

骑行现况

上海现有的自行车道是城市道路系统的一个组成部分。根据
"上海现有自行车道路"图（P68），由深蓝色逐渐变浅至浅灰色
的线条依次代表城市高速路、城市主干道、城市次干道、支路。
红色虚线为目前上海市规划的自行车禁行道路，红色为自行车单
向禁行道路。可以看到，禁行道路主要集中在上海内环线以内。[3]

　　除去骑行路线，为了了解上海中心城区各级道路骑行体验究
竟如何，我们采用了同济大学城市规划设计研究院朱玮教授团队
关于上海中心城区自行车出行环境评价的成果，并对其进行重新
整理，其中颜色越深代表评价越差（见"骑行环境评价"，
P69）。可以发现，不论是主干道、次干道，还是支路，均有骑
行体验较差的道路，并且遍布中心城区，其中以黄浦区以及虹口
区问题最为严峻（见"骑行环境评价"，P69）。[4]

3　上海市测绘院. 2016年上海道路交通管理信息图
　　[M]. 上海：上海人民出版社，2016.
4　朱玮. 上海骑行地图[DB/OL]. [2015-03-02]
　　http://zwplot.cn/Page/RideMap.html.

3　Shanghai Municipal Institute of Surveying and Mapping.
Information Map of 2016 Shanghai Road and Traffic
Management. Shanghai: Shanghai People's Publishing
House, 2016.
4　Zhu Wei. Shanghai Cycling Map. http://zwplot.cn/Page/
RideMap.html, 2015-03-02.

including nine indexes on the degree of the isolation between non-motor vehicles and motor vehicles, the volume of the bicycle lane, the flatness of the road, the density of the traffic lights, the interruption from the roadside, the afforestation, the number of motor ways (noise pollution), road-occupying and the sign of bicycles (see "Road Evaluation Criteria", p. 72 and "Evaluation Criteria Radar Chart", p. 73). After visiting all road sections and scoring them according to the standards during the field trip, the research team evaluated the road and established a database, which enabled us to compare each section based on a certain index or to locate the road section that is in worse performance according to their scores (see "Road Section Surveys", p. 70 and "Survey Result", pp. 74–83). According to current ranking of evaluated cycling lanes, we discovered that the main road and the secondary road offer better cycling experience than the branch road in general.

为进一步厘清骑行环境与道路的关系，并方便实地操作，我们制定了一份骑行体验评级表[5]，其中包含9项指标，分别为机非隔离程度、自行车道容量、路面平坦度、红绿灯密度、路侧干扰、绿化程度、周边车道数（噪声污染）、有无占道现象以及有无自行车标识（见"道路评级标准"，P72、"评级标准雷达图"，P73）。在对所有路段进行实地考查并且根据标准进行路段的评分后，我们整理出一个资料库，方便日后针对某项指标对各个路段进行比较，或根据评分的高低找出表现较差的路段（见"调研路段"，P70、"调研结果"，P74–P83）。根据现有骑行过的道路评级，团队发现，相较支路，主干道及次干道的骑行体验较好。

5　表格融合了朱玮骑行评分以及《骑行设施》(*Cycle Infrastructure*)一书的指数，并进行了简化。

5　The chart integrated and simplified the score of cycling from Zhu Wei and the index of *Cycle Infrastructure.*

上海现有自行车道路
Shanghai Existing Bicycle Lanes

——— 快速道路 High-speed road
——— 主干道 Main road
——— 次干道 Secondary road
——— 支路 Branch road
········· 自行车禁行道 Non-bicycle lanes
——— 单向自行车道 One-way cycling lanes

0 1 km

骑行环境评价
Cycling Environment Evaluation

好 Excellent
较好 Good
中 Average
较差 Fair
差 Poor
有待考察 To be investigated

资料来源：同济大学朱玮教授
Source: Professor Zhu Wei, Tongji University

0　1 km

现状研究　　　　69

─●── 调研路段 Surveyed road

0___1 km

道路评级标准
Road Evaluation Criteria

评级标准 Evaluation criteria	3分 3 points	2分 2 points	1分 1 point	0分 0 point
机非隔离程度 Isolation between non-motor vehicles and motor vehicles	绿化带 Green belt	栏杆，水泥墩子 Fence, concrete block	划线 Line	无隔离 No division
自行车道容量 The volume of the bicycle lane	大于3辆 > 3 bikes	3辆 3 bikes	2辆 2 bikes	1辆 1 bike
路面平坦度 Flatness of the road	非常高 Very good	较高 Good	较低 Low	非常低 Very low
红绿灯密度 Density of traffic light	0个/km 0/km	0-1个/km 0-1/km	1-2个/km 1-2/km	多于2个/km >2/km
路侧干扰 The interruption from the roadside	无干扰 No interruption	较低 Low	较高 High	一直干扰 Always
绿化程度 Afforestation	非常好 Very good	好 High	较低 Low	无 No
周边车道数（噪声污染） The number of motor ways (noise pollution)	无 No	单车道 Single	双车道 Double	三车道及以上 Triple or above
有无占道现象 Road-occupying	无 No	较低 Low	较高 High	非常高 Very high
有无自行车标识 Sign of bicycles	有 Yes	—	—	无 No

评级标准雷达图
Evaluation Criteria Radar Chart

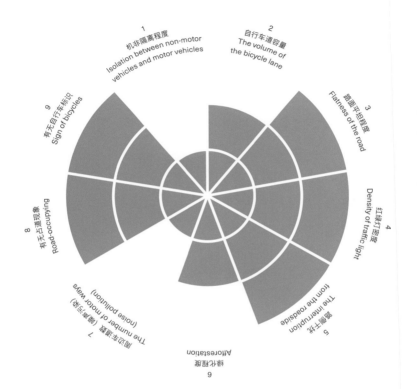

1
机非隔离程度
Isolation between non-motor vehicles and motor vehicles

2
自行车道容量
The volume of the bicycle lane

3
路面平坦程度
Flatness of the road

4
红绿灯密度
Density of traffic light

5
路侧干扰
The interruption from the roadside

6
绿化程度
Afforestation

7
同边车道数（噪声污染）
The number of motor ways (noise pollution)

8
有无占道现象
Road-occupying

9
有无自行车标识
Sign of bicycles

调研结果
Survey Result

城市主干道
City main road

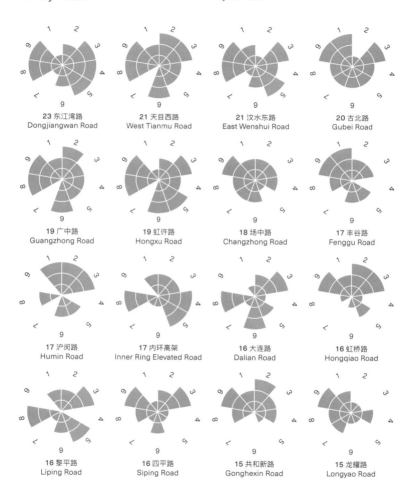

23 东江湾路
Dongjiangwan Road

21 天目西路
West Tianmu Road

21 汶水东路
East Wenshui Road

20 古北路
Gubei Road

19 广中路
Guangzhong Road

19 虹许路
Hongxu Road

18 场中路
Changzhong Road

17 丰谷路
Fenggu Road

17 沪闵路
Humin Road

17 内环高架
Inner Ring Elevated Road

16 大连路
Dalian Road

16 虹桥路
Hongqiao Road

16 黎平路
Liping Road

16 四平路
Siping Road

15 共和新路
Gonghexin Road

15 龙耀路
Longyao Road

Current Situation   74

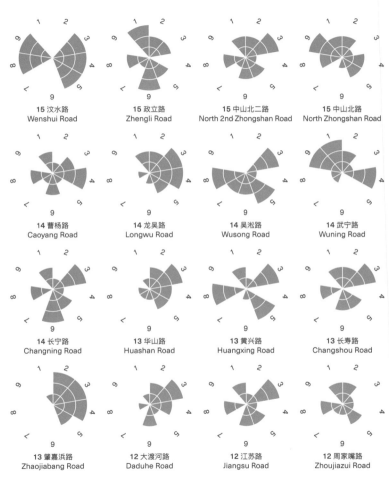

15 汶水路
Wenshui Road

15 政立路
Zhengli Road

15 中山北二路
North 2nd Zhongshan Road

15 中山北路
North Zhongshan Road

14 曹杨路
Caoyang Road

14 龙吴路
Longwu Road

14 吴淞路
Wusong Road

14 武宁路
Wuning Road

14 长宁路
Changning Road

13 华山路
Huashan Road

13 黄兴路
Huangxing Road

13 长寿路
Changshou Road

13 肇嘉浜路
Zhaojiabang Road

12 大渡河路
Daduhe Road

12 江苏路
Jiangsu Road

12 周家嘴路
Zhoujiazui Road

现状研究

11 邯郸路
Handan Road

11 军工路
Jungong Road

11 龙漕路
Longcao Road

11 徐梅路
Xumei Road

11 中环路
Middle Ring Road

10 龙华西路
West Longhua Road

9 龙华路
Longhua Road

8 宁国路
Ningguo Road

8 翔殷路
Xiangyin Road

8 延安路
Yan'an Road

7 延安西路
West Yan'an Road

7 中山南路
South Zhongshan Road

6 延安中路
Middle Yan'an Road

4 外环路
Outer Ring Road

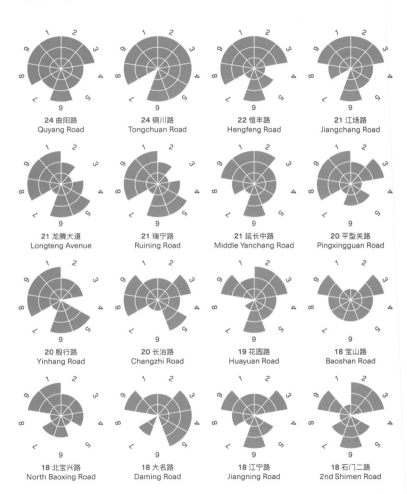

24 曲阳路
Quyang Road

24 铜川路
Tongchuan Road

22 恒丰路
Hengfeng Road

21 江场路
Jiangchang Road

21 龙腾大道
Longteng Avenue

21 瑞宁路
Ruining Road

21 延长中路
Middle Yanchang Road

20 平型关路
Pingxingguan Road

20 殷行路
Yinhang Road

20 长治路
Changzhi Road

19 花园路
Huayuan Road

18 宝山路
Baoshan Road

18 北宝兴路
North Baoxing Road

18 大名路
Daming Road

18 江宁路
Jiangning Road

18 石门二路
2nd Shimen Road

现状研究

77

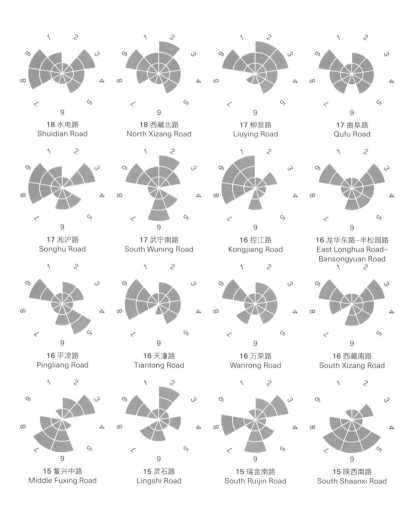

18 水电路
Shuidian Road

18 西藏北路
North Xizang Road

17 柳营路
Liuying Road

17 曲阜路
Qufu Road

17 淞沪路
Songhu Road

17 武宁南路
South Wuning Road

16 控江路
Kongjiang Road

16 龙华东路–半松园路
East Longhua Road–
Bansongyuan Road

16 平凉路
Pingliang Road

16 天潼路
Tiantong Road

16 万荣路
Wanrong Road

16 西藏南路
South Xizang Road

15 复兴中路
Middle Fuxing Road

15 灵石路
Lingshi Road

15 瑞金南路
South Ruijin Road

15 陕西南路
South Shaanxi Road

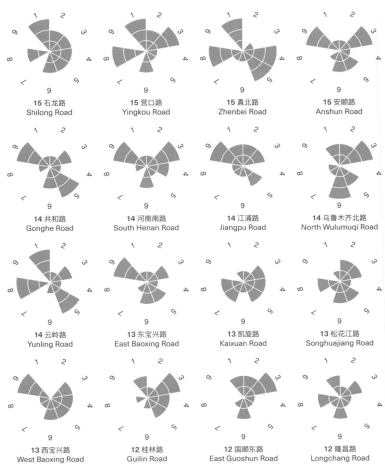

15 石龙路
Shilong Road

15 营口路
Yingkou Road

15 真北路
Zhenbei Road

15 安顺路
Anshun Road

14 共和路
Gonghe Road

14 河南南路
South Henan Road

14 江浦路
Jiangpu Road

14 乌鲁木齐北路
North Wulumuqi Road

14 云岭路
Yunling Road

13 东宝兴路
East Baoxing Road

13 凯旋路
Kaixuan Road

13 松花江路
Songhuajiang Road

13 西宝兴路
West Baoxing Road

12 桂林路
Guilin Road

12 国顺东路
East Guoshun Road

12 隆昌路
Longchang Road

现状研究

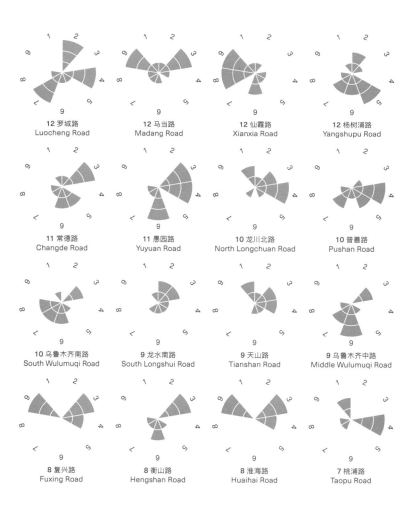

12 罗城路
Luocheng Road

12 马当路
Madang Road

12 仙霞路
Xianxia Road

12 杨树浦路
Yangshupu Road

11 常德路
Changde Road

11 愚园路
Yuyuan Road

10 龙川北路
North Longchuan Road

10 普善路
Pushan Road

10 乌鲁木齐南路
South Wulumuqi Road

9 龙水南路
South Longshui Road

9 天山路
Tianshan Road

9 乌鲁木齐中路
Middle Wulumuqi Road

8 复兴路
Fuxing Road

8 衡山路
Hengshan Road

8 淮海路
Huaihai Road

7 桃浦路
Taopu Road

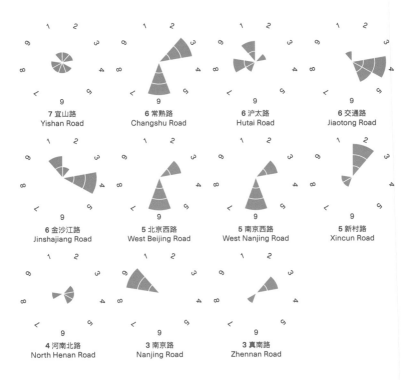

7 宜山路
Yishan Road

6 常熟路
Changshu Road

6 沪太路
Hutai Road

6 交通路
Jiaotong Road

6 金沙江路
Jinshajiang Road

5 北京西路
West Beijing Road

5 南京西路
West Nanjing Road

5 新村路
Xincun Road

4 河南北路
North Henan Road

3 南京路
Nanjing Road

3 真南路
Zhennan Road

现状研究

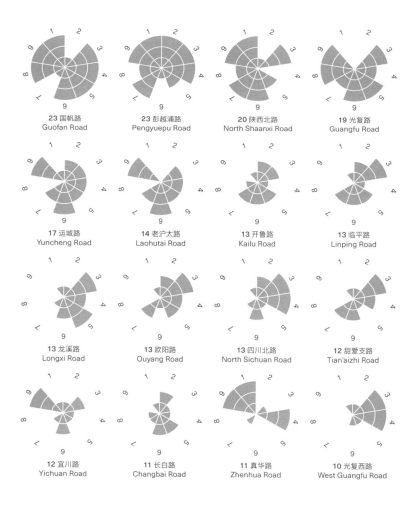

23 国帆路
Guofan Road

23 彭越浦路
Pengyuepu Road

20 陕西北路
North Shaanxi Road

19 光复路
Guangfu Road

17 运城路
Yuncheng Road

14 老沪太路
Laohutai Road

13 开鲁路
Kailu Road

13 临平路
Linping Road

13 龙溪路
Longxi Road

13 欧阳路
Ouyang Road

13 四川北路
North Sichuan Road

12 甜爱支路
Tian'aizhi Road

12 宜川路
Yichuan Road

11 长白路
Changbai Road

11 真华路
Zhenhua Road

10 光复西路
West Guangfu Road

10 宁国南路
South Ningguo Road

10 水城路
Shuicheng Road

9 公平路
Gongping Road

8 兰溪路
Lanxi Road

8 万镇路
Wanzhen Road

8 杨柳青路
Yangliuqing Road

7 杭州路
Hangzhou Road

7 华阴路
Huayin Road

6 曹安公路
Cao'an Highway

6 梅川路
Meichuan Road

4 梅岭南路
South Meiling Road

4 梅岭支路
Meiling Branch Road

4 普雄路
Puxiong Road

现状研究

案例分析 | 国际自行车友好城市
Case Study: International
Bicycle Friendly Cities

According to current map of cycling lanes, we can see that the road system in Shanghai is very complex due to multiple times of urban expansion and road renovation. How to make effective and systematic planning of cycling network? To answer this question, our team started a case study on bicycle-friendly cities all over the world. Here to list a few.

从现有骑行道路图来看，在经过多次城市扩张及道路更新后，上海道路系统已经相当庞杂，在成千上万条道路中如何进行有序、有效的骑行系统规划？为了解这一问题，我们对全球自行车友好城市进行了分析。以下为部分案例。

Copenhagen: An Example of Cycling Revival

The popularization of bicycles in Copenhagen can be traced back to the beginning of the 20th century. In 1910, Copenhagen established the first cycling lane. In the following 30 years, the number of cyclists maintained a steady growth.[1] However, in the 1950s the surge of motor vehicles in the city and the neglect of adding cycle infrastructure in new road construction dragged the rate of cycling down to the lowest 10%.[2]

The oil crisis in the 1970s and the growing environmental movement have contributed to the revival of bicycles. In order to save oil reserves, the Danish government was forced to set Sunday as Car-Free Day. At the same time, the Danish Bicycle Association organized demonstrations in Copenhagen and other cities, demanding a better bike infrastructure to enhance ride safety. These protests had made direct impact on the new urban planning, and the government has since started the construction of independent bike lanes.

With the joint efforts of the public and the government, the length of the bike lanes reached 368 km by 2014, and the cycling rate has reached to 63%.[3] Besides the commuting road, the cycling network in Copenhagen has two characteristics: First, a 110 km green corridor system is planned.

丹麦哥本哈根：复兴的案例

自行车在哥本哈根的普及可以追溯到20世纪初。1910年，哥本哈根建立了第一条自行车道。在随后的30年间，其骑行人数保持着稳定增长[1]。然而在20世纪50年代，随着城市中机动车数量的激增以及新建道路对自行车设施的忽视，到了20世纪60年代末和70年代初，自行车出行比例一度下降到了历史最低点10%。[2]

20世纪70年代，两次石油危机及日益高涨的环保运动促成了自行车的复兴。为了节约石油储备，丹麦政府被迫将周日定为"无车日"。与此同时，丹麦自行车协会在哥本哈根及其他城市组织示威游行，要求建设更好的自行车基础设施，以提升骑行的安全性。这些事件对新的城市规划产生了直接影响，由此政府开始了独立自行车道的建设。

在市民及政府的共同努力下，至2014年，哥本哈根市内的自

1　Ministry of Foreign Affairs of Denmark. *Copenhagen: Bike City for more than a century*.http://denmark.dk/en/green-living/bicycle-culture/copenhagen-bike-city-for-more-than-a-century, 2017-07-12.

2　Athlyn Cathcart-Keays. Where is the most cycle-friendly city in the world? *The Guardian*, https://www.theguardian.com/cities/2016/jan/05/where-world-most-cycle-friendly-city-amsterdam-copenhagen, 2016-01-05/2017-07-12.

1　Ministry of Foreign Affairs of Denmark. *Copenhagen: Bike City for more than a century* [R/OL]. [2017-07-12]. http://denmark.dk/en/green-living/bicycle-culture/copenhagen-bike-city-for-more-than-a-century.

2　Athlyn Cathcart-Keays. "Where is the most cycle-friendly city in the world?" [N/OL]. *The Guardian*，[2016-01-05/2017-07-12] https://www.theguardian.com/cities/2016/jan/05/where-world-most-cycle-friendly-city-amsterdam-copenhagen.

案例分析

The routes are set along the existing green lands and rivers to avoid the noisy motor vehicle lanes and to provide a good cycling experience for the citizens;[4] Second, Copenhagen has started the construction of radial bike expressways (28 expressways, 500 km) at the outskirts of the city center since 2012, which is to encourage more people to cycle into the urban areas and to reduce traffic congestion (see "Copenhagen Cycling Network", pp. 94 – 95).[5]

In addition, the bicycle-friendly characteristic is also reflected in the road design details. For example, the non-motor vehicle lanes were elevated and marked by different pavement to distinguish from the motor vehicle roads. Foot set and handrails are installed at intersections, so the cyclists can rest on it instead of on the ground when waiting for the green light (see image pp. 96 – 97). Besides, a special signal light for cyclists are set four seconds ahead than the signal for motor vehicles, so the cyclists can pass through the intersection earlier.

行车道长度达到了368 km，居民骑行出行率达到了63%[3]。除去市内沿主要道路的通勤用自行车网络系统，哥本哈根自行车系统还具备两个特点：一是规划了110 km的绿廊系统，此路线尽可能沿市内现有绿地河流及景观进行建设，以避开嘈杂的机动车线路，给骑行者提供舒适的体验[4]；二是自2012年起，哥本哈根开始在近郊建设通往市中心的辐射状的自行车快速道（28条，共计500 km），以鼓励更多市民骑行进入市区，减少拥堵（见"哥本哈根自行车道网络"，P94–P95）。[5]

　　除去规划层面的思考，自行车友好也体现在具体路段及细节设计上。例如，为了与机动车道区分，非机动车道的标高会相应抬高，并通过铺装予以标示；在路口设置脚踏及扶手，红灯时骑行者可靠在上方休息，而无需用脚勉强撑地（见"供骑行者休息的脚踏，哥本哈根"，P96–P97）。此外还特地为自行车设置交通灯，比机动车信号灯至少早5秒，这样骑行者可提前通过交叉地进入口。

3　The City of Copenhagen Technical and Environmental Administration. *Copenhagen city of cyclists: the bicycle account 2014*. http://www.cycling-embassy.dk/wp-content/uploads/2015/05/Copenhagens-Bicycle-Account-2014.pdf, 2015-05/2017-07-13.

4　Stefan Bendinks, Aglaee Degros. *Cycle Infrastructure*. Rotterdam: Nai010, 2013: 44-51.

5　Ministry of Foreign Affairs of Denmark. *Cycle Super Highway*. http://denmark.dk/en/green-living/bicycle-culture/cycle-super-highway, 2017-07-13.

3　The City of Copenhagen Technical and Environmental Administration Mobility and Urban Space. Copehagen city of cyclists: the bicycle account 2014 [R/OL]. [2015-05/2017-07-13] http://www.cycling-embassy.dk/wp-content/uploads/2015/05/Copenhagens-Bicycle-Account-2014.pdf.

4　Stefan Bendinks, Aglaee Degros. Cycle Infrastructure [M]. Rotterdam: Nai010, 2013: 44-51.

5　Ministry of Foreign Affairs of Denmark. Cycle Super Highway [R/OL]. http://denmark.dk/en/green-living/bicycle-culture/cycle-super-highway, 2017-07-13.

哥本哈根自行车道网络
Copenhagen Cycling Network

Frederiksborgvej

16

211

Slotsherrensvej

Jyllingevej

腓特烈斯贝
Frederiksberg

Peter Bangs Vej

02

151

E20

——— 自行车主干道 Primary cycling routes
------- 自行车支路 Secondary cycling routes
——— 长途自行车道 Long-distance cycling routes

Case Study   94

gen ···· 152

Amager Strandvej

Amagerbrogade

Englandsvej

Ørestads Blvd

0 _____ 1 km

案例分析   95

供骑行者休憩的脚踏，哥本哈根
Foot set for cyclists, Copenhagen

Rotterdam: Multi-Layered Cycling Network

The Rotterdam government has always attached high attention on the construction of cycle infrastructure. As the largest port city in Europe, Rotterdam built an underwater tunnel in Maas Harbor in 1942 to connect the north and south sides of the city and reduce the influence to the sailing, which includes two side-by-side motorways, a sidewalk and a bike lane. By 1950, the volume of bicycles passing through the tunnel once reached 40,000. Although there are several bridges built over the River Maas in the following decades to relieve some traffic flow, 4,500 bikes are still passing through the tunnel every day.[6]

From the planning of the Rotterdam Municipal Government (2010), Rotterdam's existing urban cycle network can be divided into three layers.

The first layer is the main cycle routes, which is about 3 km to 12 km. It is mainly connected to the city's public center and the transportation points (such as the theatre in the south of the plaza, the city center and Alexander Train Station). The goal is to help the cyclists to cross the city and arrive their destinations quickly.

The second layer is the regional roads. Their network density is about 1 km to 1.5 km, and has been further refined into 0.5 km to 1 km considering

荷兰鹿特丹：多层次的自行车道路网

鹿特丹政府向来重视自行车设施建设。作为欧洲最大的港口城市，为了连接城市南北两侧并且避免影响海船进出港，早在1942年，鹿特丹就在马斯港建设了一条水下隧道，其中包括两条并排机动车道（2车道×2车道），一条人行道及一条自行车道。至1950年，隧道内自行车使用量曾一度达到40 000辆次。尽管在随后的几十年间，马斯河上新建了不少桥梁，它们承担了部分流量，但隧道内每天依然有4 500辆次自行车经过。[6]

从鹿特丹市政府的2010年规划来看，鹿特丹现有的城市自行车网络大致可分为三级。

第一级为城市自行车干道，相对应的骑行距离约为3~12 km，主要连接城市公共中心及各交通节点（如南剧院、市中心、亚力山大火车站），目标是帮助骑行者快速穿越城市抵达目的地。

[6] Mark Wagenbuur. Maastunnel Rotterdam [EB/OL]. [2011-03-29/2017-07-13]. https://bicycledutch.wordpress.com/2011/03/29/maastunnel-rotterdam/.

6 Mark Wagenbuur. Maastunnel Rotterdam. https://bicycledutch.wordpress.com/2011/03/29/maastunnel-rotterdam/, 2011-03-29/2017-07-13.

the group of cyclists is larger in part of the regions. This grid in such density ensures that residents can reach the planned cycle path within the range of 250 m to 500 m.

The third layer linked Rotterdam and the surrounding landscape together, whose function is for commuting and entertaining at the same time. The bike network crossed the viaduct of Hofplein, and was extended to the Zuiderpark and IJsselmonde area along the river. It is also stretching to the port in the west along River Maas, which is the main industrial area in Rotterdam (see "Rotterdam Cycling Network", pp. 102 – 103).[7]

第二级是区域型道路，设计网络密度为1~1.5 km。考虑部分区域骑行者数量较多，网格有时被进一步细化至0.5~1 km。这样的网格密度保证了居民在250~500 m范围内就能使用到规划的自行车道。

　　第三级是将鹿特丹与周围景观联系在一起的骑行道路，它兼具通勤与休闲的双重功能。这个自行车网络穿过霍夫波莱恩的高架桥，沿着河流到达南部公园和艾瑟尔蒙德地区，同时还沿着马斯河向西部的港口区延伸，这里是鹿特丹主要的工业区（见"鹿特丹自行车道网络"，P102–P103）。[7]

7　Gemeente Rotterdam. ActiePlan Rotterdam Fietsts [R/OL]. [2017-07-13] http://www.fietsberaad.nl/library/repository/bestanden/actieplanFiets%20rotterdam.pdf.

7　Gemeente Rotterdam. ActiePlan Rotterdam Fietsts. http://www.fietsberaad.nl/library/repository/bestanden/actieplanFiets%20rotterdam.pdf, 2017-07-13.

鹿特丹自行车道网络
Rotterdam Cycling Network

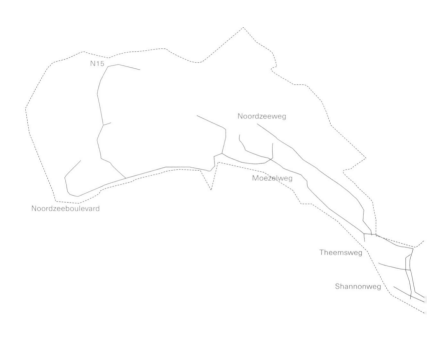

N15

Noordzeeweg

Moezelweg

Noordzeeboulevard

Theemsweg

Shannonweg

—— 自行车道 Cycling routes
河道 Canals

马斯隧道里的骑行者，鹿特丹(1966)
Cyclists in Maastunnel, Rotterdam, 1966

Berlin: Independent and Various Cycling System

Berlin is the biggest bicycle-friendly city with 891.85 km² (4 times the central area of Shanghai). It is also a typical case for slow traffic system. After the first cycle lane to the downtown was opened in 2005, the city has 620 km of cycle lanes until 2008, including 150 km bicycle lane, 190 km off-road cycling lane and 100 km lane shared by both cyclists and pedestrians. After introducing the "calm zone", the speed of the motor vehicle was limited to 30 km/h, which has indirectly improved the cycling experience. According to the media report, the cyclists has reached to 0.5 million per day in 2013, which means 710 out of every 1,000 citizens will have their own bicycles.[8]

In Berlin, the cycling system is composed of four layers, including the cycling route along Berlin Wall, the long distance cycling route, the main cycling route and the branch cycling route. The long-distance bike lane is in radial form, connecting Berlin with the surrounding cities, such as Copenhagen and the Euroroute R1.

德国柏林：独立而丰富的自行车系统

柏林现为面积最大的自行车友好城市，面积达到了891.85 km²（是上海中心城区面积的4倍），为大型城市推行慢行系统的典型案例。自2005年第一条通往市中心的自行车道开通后，到2008年，柏林已经拥有了620 km的自行车道，其中包括150 km的自行车专用道、190 km的越野自行车道，以及100 km的自行车、行人共用道。在引入"限声区"策略后，机动车速度被限制在30 km/h以下，该策略间接地提升了骑行体验。据媒体报道，2013年柏林每天骑自行车的人数就已达50万人，每1 000个柏林市民中就有710人拥有自己的自行车。[8]

柏林的自行车道系统分为四个层级：沿柏林墙自行车道、长途自行车道、自行车主干道及自行车支路。长途自行车道呈放射状，将柏林与周边城市进行连接，如哥本哈根、欧洲自行车道R1。

8   Megan Arellano. Lessons From Biking in Berlin [R/OL]. Planet Froward, [2012-11-01/2017-07-13]. http://www.planetforward.org/2012/11/01/lessons-from-biking-in-berlin.

8   Megan Arellano. Lessons From Biking in Berlin. Planet Froward, http://www.planetforward.org/2012/11/01/lessons-from-biking-in-berlin, 2012-11-01/2017-07-13.

12 main cycle routes are also extended in radical pattern, and form a spider web with eight ring roads. The branch cycle routes subdivide the system based on this structure (see "Berlin Cycling Network", pp. 110 – 111).

After comparing the cycling route and rail system in Berlin, we found they share similar structure, but independent and different with each other in many routes. Cycling is not a supplement of rail traffic in Berlin, but an independent system.

It is worth mentioning that although the planning of public transportation does not emphasize the connection with cycle routes, most rails allow bicycles and would make a mark on the cabin, which is similar in the Netherlands. [9]

12条自行车主干道亦呈放射状，其间配合8条环状道路形成蛛网型架构（见"柏林自行车道网络"，P110–P111）。自行车支路则在此系统基础上进一步细分。

比对柏林自行车道与地铁线路，我们发现柏林的地铁线路与自行车的主干道具有相似的放射趋势，但两者大部分线路不吻合，分别以各自完整的系统单独运作。自行车系统在柏林并不只是作为地铁交通的补充，而是一个独立的系统。

值得一提的是，尽管在线路规划上并不强调公共交通与自行车衔接，但柏林的大多数轨道交通都允许自行车上车，并在相应的车厢外标示自行车标识，这一做法与荷兰相似。[9]

9 Senate Department for Urban Development.
   Cycling in Berlin [R/OL]. Berlin.de,
   [2017-07-13]. https://web.archive.org/web/
   20080224095002/, http://www.
   stadtentwicklung.berlin.de:80/verkehr/
   radverkehr/index_en.shtml.

9 Senate Department for Urban Development. Cycling in Berlin. Berlin.de, https://web.archive.org/web/20080224095002/http://www.stadtentwicklung.berlin.de:80/verkehr/radverkehr/index_en.shtml, 2017-07-13.

柏林自行车道网络
Berlin Cycling Network

RR 5
奥拉宁堡
Oranienburg

RR 4
亨尼希斯多夫
Hennigsdorf

TR

TR 6
TR 5

柏林–哥本哈根蝶
Berlin-Kopenhagen
Havel-Radweg
Königin-Luise-Route

Havelland 骑行道
Havelland-Radweg

RR 3
法尔肯塞
Falkensee

Spree 骑行道
Spree-Radweg

TR 2

RR 2
Gross-Glienicke

TR 5

TR 4

TR

TR 8

Europaradweg R 1
D-Route 3
Havel 骑行道
Havel-Radweg

RR 1
波茨坦
Potsdam

RR 12
泰尔托
Teltow

RR
马
Ma

------ 自行车主干道 Primary cycling routes
  ●   主干道节点 Primary cycling nodes
------ 自行车支路 Secondary cycling routes
------ 长途自行车道 Long-distance cycling routes
------ 柏林墙车道 Cycling routes along Berlin Wall

RR 6
贝尔瑙
Bernau
柏林–乌瑟多姆洺
Berlin-Usedom

TR 3

TR 2

TR 7 RR 7
阿伦斯费尔德
Ahrensfelde

TR 6

RR 8
霍珀加滕
Hoppegarten

TR 4

TR 8

TR 3

TR 7

Dahme-Radweg

RR 9
Erkner
D-Route 3
Spree-Radweg
Europaradweg R 1

林–莱比锡
rlin-Leipzig

RR 10
Eichwalde

达默骑行道
Dahme-Radweg

0   2 km

案例分析   111

柏林墙下的骑行者
Cyclist in front of the Berlin Wall

Vienna: the Revival of the Street

In 1980, in order to improve the quality of urban public space and stimulate the vitality of the streets, the Vienna City Council put the cycle route construction on the agenda. Six years later, Vienna has built a 168-km bicycle path. It is extended along the Donau and mainly serves for the tourist area. In 1993, the City Council proposed a new plan, hoping to raise the cycling rate up to 6% (Vienna's cycling rate is quite low compared to other European cities).[10] A year later, the first edition of cycling system planning was realized, in which 27 basic cycle lanes were designed for daily commuting and leisure. This plan has also laid solid foundation for the future development.

In 2003, the Government of Vienna began to increase the budget for the construction of cycle infrastructure, which has promoted the further development of bicycle infrastructure. Based on the original design, the system was further subdivided. By 2013, all districts are equipped with bicycles.

The Donau divided Vienna into two parts, and important buildings are concentrated in the south bank, which has been somehow reflected by the cycle routes planning. Both sides of the Donau were designed

奥地利维也纳：街道活力的再现

1980年，为了改善城市公共空间品质，激发街道活力，维也纳市议会将自行车道路修建提上日程。6年后，168 km的自行车道在维也纳修建完工，车道沿多瑙河，以服务旅游区为主。1993年，市议会提出一项新的规划建议，将骑行出行比例提升到6%（相较欧洲其他城市，维也纳骑行出行率非常低）[10]。一年后，第一版自行车道系统规划成型，规划设计了27条基本自行车道供日常通勤及休闲使用，此版规划为其后的发展铺实了基础。

　　2003年，维也纳政府开始提高自行车设施建设的预算，这一政策推动了自行车基础设施的全面发展。在原有的设计基础之上，路网被进一步细分。2013年，实现自行车各区域路网覆盖。

　　在研究维也纳自行车道规划后可以发现，多瑙河将维也纳一分为二，重要建筑均集中于南岸，这一特点在其自行车系统规划

10　Vienna City Administration. Historische Entwicklung des Wiener Radverkehrsnetzes [R/OL]. Wien.at, [2017-07-13] https://www.wien.gv.at/stadtentwicklung/projekte/verkehrsplanung/radwege/historie.html.

10　Vienna City Administration. Historische Entwicklung des Wiener Radverkehrsnetzes. Wien.at,https://www.wien.gv.at/stadtentwicklung/projekte/verkehrsplanung/radwege/historie.html, 2017-07-13.

with landscape cycle lanes, and are connected by the bridge. Following the ring road encircling the city, the cycle lane starts from the city center and connects all major buildings, extending outward along the current network of roads (see "Vienna Cycling Network", pp. 118 – 119).[11]

中可见一二。多瑙河两侧沿岸均设计了景观骑行道，通过桥梁实现两岸的连接。市中心的自行车道则沿着环城大道，连接各个主要建筑，并随现有路网呈辐射状向外扩散（见"维也纳自行车道网络"，P118-P119）。[11]

11 Stefan Bendinks, Aglaee Degros.
Cycle Infrastructure [M]. Rotterdam: Nai010,
2013: 93-99.

11 Stefan Bendinks, Aglaee Degros. Cycle Infrastructure.
Rotterdam: Nai010, 2013: 93-99.

維也納自行車道網絡
Vienna Cycling Network

Heiligenstädter Strasse

Dona
Autob

Krottenbachstrasse

Hauptstrasse

Ketzergasse

Laxenburgerstrasse

——— 1992年建成自行车道
Cycling routes completed in 1992
- - - 2000年建成自行车道
Cycling routes completed in 2000
········ 2013年建成自行车道
Cycling routes completed in 2013

Case Study   118

B7

Friedhofweg

多瑙河
Donau

Esslinger Hauptstrasse

Auernheimergasse

Ost Autobahn

B225

Klederinger Strasse

B16

机场
Airport

0 ___ 1 km

Paris: Equal Importance on Metro and Cycling System

Paris has been building cycle lanes since the beginning of the 1990s and has completed 700 km cycle lanes by 2015, including independent cycle lanes and the ones based on widened roads. In Paris, the population density is around 22,000 people/km², which is close to that of Shanghai's city center.[12]

In fact Paris has a very well-developed metro system. If we draw a 500 m purple radius circle around each metro station, we can find that most area of Paris is covered by these purple circles, which means most citizens will be able to access to a metro station within 500 m (see "Paris Metro System and Service Area", pp. 124 – 125).

However, even with such convenient subway system, Paris keeps the construction of its cycle lanes. In April 2015, the Paris government announced to increase the length of the bike path to 1400 km by 2020, with additional 10,000 bicycle parking lots. In the planning, the cycle lane network in Paris has three layers, including the express way, the main road and branch road. The express way consists of four lines, mainly in east-west direction and another two north- south direction along the two banks of the Seine River. The main road is encircling the city center of Paris

法国巴黎：地铁系统与自行车道并重

从20世纪90年代开始，巴黎开始修建自行车道系统。到2015年，巴黎已经建设了700km的自行车道，其中包括独立专用道及在原有道路上拓宽后的自行车道。巴黎的人口密度为22 000人/km²，与上海中心城区的人口密度相当接近。[12]

事实上巴黎拥有非常完善的地铁系统，我们将巴黎的地铁站用紫色的点表示出来，然后以点为中心画半径为500m的浅紫色圆，可以看到浅紫色圆覆盖了大部分的巴黎，这也意味着在大多数情况下，巴黎市民在500m内就能到达某一个地铁站（见"巴黎地铁系统及其服务半径"，P124-P125）。

然而，即使拥有如此便利的地铁系统，巴黎仍然在继续推动自行车道的建设。2015年4月，巴黎政府宣布，计划在2020年将巴黎的自行车道长度增加至1 400公里，同时增设10 000个自行

12 Elizabeth Pineau. *Paris: from tyranny of taxis to city of bikes*. https://www.theglobeandmail.com/life/paris-from-tyranny-of-taxis-to-city-of-bikes/article1670498/, 2010-08-12/2017-07-13.

12 Elizabeth Pineau. Paris: from tyranny of taxis to city of bikes [N/OL]. the global and mail, [2010-08-12/2017-07-13]. https://www.theglobeandmail.com/life/paris-from-tyranny-of-taxis-to-city-of-bikes/article1670498/.

in three circles from inside out; the branch roads for bicycles are crossing through the blank areas inside the network (see "Paris Cycling Network", pp. 126 – 127).[13,14]

In addition, the bike lane system in Paris has strong connection with the city's green space as well as the famous buildings. It is obvious that the bike works not only as a commuting tool, but a way of experiencing Paris, representing the identity of Paris with many other different landscapes (see "Paris Cycling Network, Green Space, and Famous Building", pp. 128 – 129).

车停车场。规划中，巴黎自行车道网路分为三层：快速道，主干道及支路。快速道由四条路线组成，主要分为东西、南北两条轴，沿塞纳河两岸各置一条。主干道由内而外三圈环绕巴黎市中心。自行车支路则穿插于网络空白处（见"巴黎自行车道网络"，P126–P127）。[13, 14]

　　此外，我们发现，巴黎的自行车道系统与城市中的著名建筑与绿地之间有着紧密的联系，自行车道或途经，或连接起著名建筑，在大型绿地中也密布着自行车道路网（见"巴黎自行车道网络，绿地及著名建筑"，P128–P129）。由此可知，在公共交通发达的巴黎，自行车已经不仅是一种通勤工具，而且与众多景观结合成一个系统，共同提升着巴黎的城市形象。

13　France24. *Paris plans to become "world cycling capital"*. http://www.france24.com/en/20150405-paris-cycling-world-capital-pollution, 2014-03-11/2017-07-13.

14　Bikes to Rule Paris. bicyclenetwork, https://www.bicyclenetwork.com.au/general/policy-and-campaigns/2684/.

13　France24. Paris plans to become "world cycling capital" [N/OL]. [2014-03-11/2017-07-13] http://www.france24.com/en/20150405-paris-cycling-world-capital-pollution.

14　Bikes to Rule Paris [N/OL]. bicyclenetwork, [2015-04-21/2017-07-13] https://www.bicyclenetwork.com.au/general/policy-and-campaigns/2684/.

巴黎地铁系统及其服务半径
Paris Metro System and Service Area

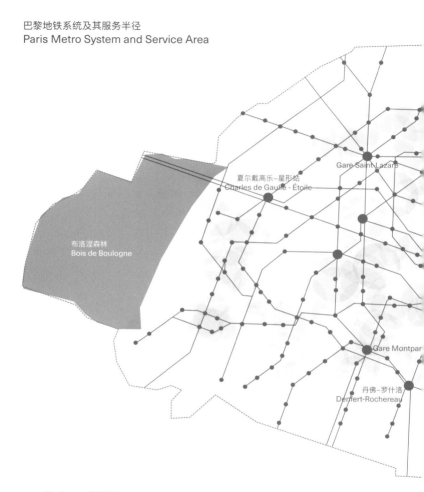

Service area 服务半径
● Metro station 地铁站点
—— Metro line 地铁线

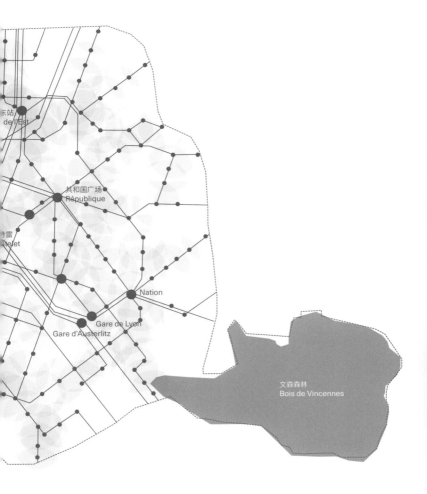

东站
de l'Est

共和国广场
République

夏特雷
Châtelet

Nation

Gare de Lyon
Gare d'Austerlitz

文森森林
Bois de Vincennes

0   1 km

案例分析   125

巴黎自行车道网络
Paris Cycling Network

Boulevards
des Maréchaux

罗什舒阿尔
Boulevard de Rochechouart

N185

布洛涅森林
Bois de Boulogne

圣日耳曼德佩
Boulevard
Saint-Germain

奥古斯特布朗基辉
Boulevard
Auguste Blanqui

Parc des Rives de Seine

Port de Javel Bas

Boulevards des Maréchaux

Avenue du Général Leclerc

—— 自行车快速道 Fast cycling routes
—— 自行车主干道 Primary cycling routes
—— 自行车支路 Secondary cycling routes

欧贝维利耶
Rue d'Aubervilliers

贝尔维尔
Boulevard de Belleville

博马舍
Boulevard
Beaumarchais

勒努瓦
Boulevard
Richard Lenoir

D120

文森森林
Bois de Vincennes

Port de Bercy
Port de Tolbiac

0   1 km

巴黎自行车道网络，绿地及著名建筑
Paris Cycling Network, Green Spaces, and Famous Buildings

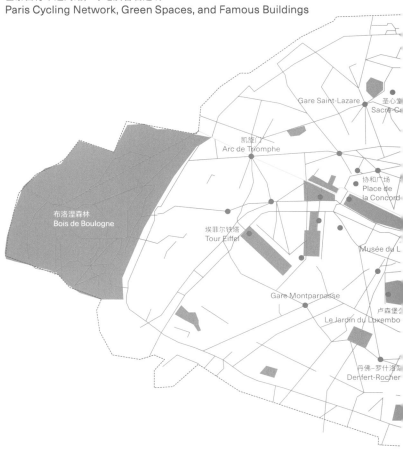

—— 自行车道 Cycling network
■ 绿地 Green space
● 著名建筑 Famous building

共和国广场
République

Gare de Lyon

文森森林
Bois de Vincennes

0 _____ 1 km

Nantes, France: A Combination of Cycling Routes and Natural Landscape

250 km rivers, 100 parks, 485 km cycle lanes, 9 cycle lanes with natural landscape that is longer than 10 km to 40 km...,[15-17] these figures has brought the name "European Green Capital" to the city of Nantes in 2013. The city was also listed in the Copehagenize Index for three consecutive years. Since the city is in quite small scale, transportation only plays a supporting role in Nantes. There are only three tram rails by now (see "Nantes Cycling Network and Tram System", pp. 132 – 133).[18, 19]

法国南特：骑行网络和自然景观的融合

250 km河流、100个公园、485 km骑行道、9条10~40 km以上的自然景观骑行线路[15-17]……这一系列数据让法国南特在2013年被提名为"欧洲绿都"，并且连续三年名列哥本哈根自行车友好城市榜单。由于城市规模较小，相比其他城市，公共交通在此仅起到辅助作用，迄今为止，仅修建了3条电车线路（见"南特自行车道网络及电车系统"，P132–P133）。[18, 19]

15 *Nantes by Bike. France Velo Tourism*, http://en. francevelotourisme.com/base-1/destinations/nantes-velo-tourisme/troncons/nantes-velo-tourisme, 2017-07-14.

16 *Carte des continuités et pistes cyclables*. http://www. nantesmetropole.fr/pratique/deplacements/carte-des-continuites-et-pistes-cyclables-52443.kjsp?RH=WEB, 2017-07-14.

17 Destination "Nantes Vélo Tourisme." https://www. francevelotourisme.com/base-1/destinations/nantes-velo-tourisme, 2017-7-14.

18 High quality of life in a European Green Capital. Official website of the city of Nantes, http://en.nantes.fr/home/green-capital.html, 2017-07-14.

19 Tramway de Nantes. Wikipedia, https://fr.wikipedia.org/wiki/Tramway_de_Nantes, 2017-07-14.

15 Nantes by Bike [EB/OL]. France Velo Tourism, [2017-07-14]. http://en.francevelotourisme.com/base-1/destinations/nantes-velo-tourisme/troncons/nantes-velo-tourisme.

16 Carte des continuités et pistes cyclables [DB/OL]. [2017-07-14]. http://www. nantesmetropole.fr/pratique/deplacements/carte-des-continuites-et-pistes-cyclables-52443.kjsp?RH=WEB.

17 Destination "Nantes Vélo Tourisme" [DB/OL]. [2017-7-14]. https://www.francevelotourisme.com/base-1/destinations/nantes-velo-tourisme.

18 High quality of life in a European Green Capital [R/OL]. Official website of the city of Nantes, [2017-07-14]. http://en.nantes.fr/home/green-capital.html.

19 Tramway de Nantes. [DB/OL]. [2017-07-14]. https://fr.wikipedia.org/wiki/Tramway_de_Nantes.

南特自行车道网络及电车系统
Nantes Cycling Network and Tram System

Chemin de la Justice

2号有轨电车
Tram 2

Bd Albert Einstein

Bd Robert Schuman

3号有轨电车
Tram 3

Bd Jean Ingres

Rue du Corps de Garde

Rue de la Durantière

1号有轨电车
Tram 1

Bd Bâtonnier Cholet

Rue des Usines

—— 自行车主干道 Primary cycling routes
—— 自行车道（与公交，行人共用）
Cycling routes (shared with public
transportation and pedestrian)
—— 电车道 Tram routes
·········· 规划电车道 Planned tram routes

Route de Gachet

Bd des Européens

Route de Saint-Joseph
Route de Carquefou

1号有轨电车
Tram 1

Route de Sainte-Luce

Bd de la Prairie de Mauves

有轨电车
ram 2&3

Bd Joliot Curie

Bd de Vendée

0   1 km

案例分析   133

Dublin: Multidimensional Cycling Network

As the number of cyclists keeps growing, Dublin proposed the 2024 planning on cycling network in 2014. Under this plan that envisions to expand the 500 km network to 2,840 km. The National Transportation Commission expected to allow 75,000 people to ride a bike every morning in the future.[20]

The Dublin's cycle network is more mixed than other cities. The system consists of four layers (see "Dublin Cycling Network", pp. 136 – 137 and "Dublin Landscape Cycling Network", pp. 138 – 139):

1. Landscape cycle route along the green land and river;
2. Main cycle routes that connect the major event centers;
3. Long-distance cycle routes that connect the suburb with the city center;
4. Branch bicycle lanes of different densities.[21]

爱尔兰都柏林：多维骑行网络

由于骑行人数不断增长，2014年，都柏林提出2024年骑行网络的规划。计划将总长500 km的网络扩张至2 840 km。国家交通委员会希望通过此计划能让75 000人骑上自行车通勤。[20]

相比其他城市，都柏林的自行车网络系统较为混杂，由四个层级组成（见"都柏林自行车道网络"，P136–P137、"都柏林景观自行车道网络"，P138–P139）：

1. 沿绿地河流的景观骑行道；
2. 连接城市主要活动中心的自行车主干道；
3. 连接周边与市中心的长途自行车道；
4. 不同密度的自行车支路。[21]

20 Rónán Duffy. These maps show the planned 2,840 km of cycle routes for the greater Dublin area. the journal.ie, http://www.thejournal.ie/dublin-cycling-plan-1410242-Apr2014/, 2014-04-11/2017-07-13.

21 National Transport Authority. Greater Dublin Area Cycle Network Plan, http://www.nationaltransport.ie/wp-content/uploads/2014/04/Proposed_Network_Dublin.pdf, 2014-04/2017-07-13.

20 Rónán Duffy. These maps show the planned 2,840 km of cycle routes for the greater Dublin area [N/OL]. the journal.ie, [2014-04-11/2017-07-13]. http://www.thejournal.ie/dublin-cycling-plan-1410242-Apr2014/.

21 National Transport Authority. Greater Dublin Area Cycle Network Plan, [2014-04/2017-07-13]. http://www.nationaltransport.ie/wp-content/uploads/2014/04/Proposed_Network_Dublin.pdf.

都柏林自行车道网络
Dublin Cycling Network

邓博因
Dunboyne

克洛尼
Clonee

莱克斯利普
Leixlip

卢肯
Lucan

拉斯库尔
Rathcoole

Ballinascorney

基尔蒂尔
Kilteel

—— 自行车主干道 Primary cycling routes
—— 自行车支路 Secondary cycling routes
—— 长途自行车道 Long-distance cycling routes

柏林机场
blin Airport

波特马诺克
Portmarnock

霍斯
Howth

都柏林湾
Dublin Bay

brook

Stepaside

Carrickmines

0 _____ 2 km

都柏林景观自行车道网络
Dublin Landscape Cycling Network

克洛尼
Clonee

莱克斯利普
Leixlip

凤凰公园
Phoenix Park

克朗多金
Clondalkin

Ballinascorney

■ 绿地 Green space
—— 滨河自行车道 Riverside cycling routes
—— 绿地自行车道 Green cycling routes

波特马诺克
Portmarnock

霍斯
Howth

都柏林湾
Dublin Bay

Howth

brook

Bray

Stepaside

0   2 km

Conclusion: Systematic Planning and Infrastructure Construction

In the case study of 7 bicycle-friendly cities, you can find out that no matter it is Copenhagen and Rotterdam which have a long history of cycling, or Paris and Vienna which have newly become bike-friendly cities, they all have been continuing the construction of cycle infrastructure based on their own character in the past twenty years, and have brought up positive achievements, for example, the cycling becomes more efficient and less time-consuming, and cycling itself has also become part of the city's culture. According to the latest poll result and the actual results of the assessment, these cities also have new requirement for the future development of cycling network and infrastructure.

In contrast, the cycling in Shanghai has been enslaved to the outdated infrastructure and few systematic planning. If Shanghai wants to develop into a bike-friendly city in the future and improve the citizens' quality of life, the primary task is to plan the cycling system and gradually build the infrastructure.

结论：整体规划和基础设施建设

在7座自行车友好城市的案例研究中，可以发现不管是有着骑行传统的哥本哈根和鹿特丹，还是近年来逐渐进入自行车友好城市行列的巴黎和维也纳，它们都在近二十多年间根据自身特点和目标持续进行自行车设施的基础建设，而这些努力也颇见成效：出行时间成本降低，骑行出行率提高，骑行本身也逐渐成为城市文化的一部分。根据最新的民调结果及实际效果评估，这些城市对未来自行车网络的发展和设施又提出了新一轮的要求。

　　反观上海近年来骑行所遇到的主要问题，正是受制于设施陈旧而未经设计的现状，现有的自行车道缺乏系统的规划和思考。上海倘若希望在未来发展成为自行车友好城市，提升市民生活品质，其首要任务就是对现有非机动车道系统进行合理规划，并逐步改善基础设施。

系统规划｜骑行上海
System Planning:
Cycling@Shanghai

How to apply the current planning strategy of bicycle-friendly city to the cycling of Shanghai? How to make reasonable planning and to carry out the infrastructure construction based on the characters of Shanghai itself? After comparing the planning of different cycling-friendly cities, we found the planned cycling network has multiple layers, and each layer has its specific character to solve different issues.

There are green cycling routes along the landscape to improve the cycling experience (e.g. Copenhagen and Dublin); commuting cycling routes that connected different city hubs (e.g. Rotterdam, Vienna and Paris); express routes that are exclusive for cyclists to ride from peri-urban areas to the city center (e.g. Copenhagen and Berlin); cycling networks that change in density with the growth of cyclists (e.g. Rotterdam and Vienna). Among them, Dublin is a typical sample with clearer structure. Comparing these cities with Shanghai, we believe that the cycling system in Shanghai should be composed of three layers: green cycling routes for the public to exercise and entertain; commuting system that links different city hubs; and the "last kilometer" system that supplement the current rail transportation.

如何运用现有自行车友好城市的规划思路进行上海骑行系统的设计？如何针对上海城市本身特点进行合理的规划并实施自行车基础设施建设？在对比了各自行车友好城市的规划后，我们发现其骑行系统通常由多套系统重叠构成，每个系统都有其不同侧重点，以解决不同类型的出行难题。

例如，有结合绿地景观提升骑行体验的自行车绿道（如哥本哈根、都柏林）；有连接城市公共中心的自行车通勤干道（如鹿特丹、维也纳、巴黎）；有专供骑行者从周边抵达市中心的快速道路（如哥本哈根、柏林）；也有区域网格密度会根据骑行者数量增多而进行细化(如鹿特丹、维也纳)；而都柏林，则是诸多案例中典型的结构较清晰的代表。相应地，考虑到上海中心城区与这些城市的异同，我们认为上海骑行系统应当由三个层级组成：供市民休闲健身的绿廊系统，连接城市公共中心的通勤系统，以及配合现有轨道交通出行的"最后一公里"系统。

Green Cycling Routes

Similar to the landscape cycling routes in Copenhagen, Berlin and Nantes, we first proposed a green cycling system to combine the current park land and river landscape in Shanghai to further enhance the urban cycling experience and to provide daily entertainment for the citizens. To find out the appropriate green corridors, we first studied current green spaces and landscape system in Shanghai. According to the documents from Shanghai Planning and Land Resource Administration Bureau and the website of Shanghai Federation of Labor, the green land system is developed in the format of "core, ring, corridor, wedge and network", and the green coverage ratio has reached 38%, allowing 12.5 m² public green land per person. However, when checking the layout of urban ecological land use, we discovered that most of the large-scale continuous green lands are in Pudong or outside the outer ring road.[1]

The public green spaces in the center areas in Shanghai are very small and fragmented, which makes it difficult to simply apply the European approaches, for example, using large green spaces that are 1 km to 2 km long as the foundation for green route development. Therefore, the key of the green route system is to figure out a logical way to link these fragmented

绿廊系统

与哥本哈根、柏林、南特的景观自行车道相似，我们首先构想的绿廊系统旨在结合上海现有的公园绿地和河流景观，提升城市骑行体验，并可供市民日常休闲健身。为了寻找合适的绿廊，我们首先对上海现有绿地及景观系统进行了研究。根据上海市规划和国土资源管理局及上海总工会官网资料，上海绿地系统以"核、环、廊、楔、网"的布局模式发展，绿化覆盖率达38%，人均公共绿地为12.5 m²。然而，我们在查看市域生态用地布局图时却发现，上海大面积的、成规模的连续绿地大多分布在浦东，或者外环以外。[1]

上海中心城区的公共绿地面积小而零散，无法简单套用欧洲自行车友好城市的做法，即利用延绵1~2 km的大型公共绿地作为绿廊规划基础。因此，寻找合适的逻辑串联起零散的景观成为上海绿廊系统的重点。针对这个问题，我们进行了三方面的考虑。

1　上海市规划和国土资源管理局. 关于上海市基本生态网络规划主要内容的公示 [R/OL]. [2010-12-02/2017-07-14]. http://www.shgtj.gov.cn/hdpt/gzcy/sj/201012/t20101202_424485.html.

1　Shanghai Planning and Land Resource Administration Bureau. Notice on Major Content of Basic Ecological Network Planning in Shanghai. http://www.shgtj.gov.cn/hdpt/gzcy/sj/201012/t20101202_424485.html.

green lands in Shanghai. Our team studies this problem through three different aspects:

First, considering the fitness needs of residents in various districts of Shanghai, we planned internal green cycling routes to connect the key green spaces in each districts. We also plan to strengthen the landscape along the routes to help the residents to relax when cycling (see "Internal Green Cycling Routes", p. 152).

Second, we planned six long-distance green cycle routes to connect the outer green spaces with the green lands in the city center, forming cycling roads toward the downtown area. The cyclists can also take a rest when cycling through the parks (see "Long Distance Green Cycling Routes", p. 153).

In the end, we designed two river bank cycling routes along the Suzhou River and the Huangpu River, then the cyclists can enjoy the views of the riverbank when cycling (see "Riverside Cycling Routes", p. 154).

By adding these three layers together, we finalized the planning of the green route system. It will integrate the fragmented green lands, which will not only improve the experience of cycling, but also strengthen the continuity of the public green spaces in the city center (see "Complete Green Cycling Network", p. 155).

首先，考虑到上海各区居民的健身需求，规划区域内部自行车绿廊（见"区域内部自行车绿廊"，P152），将每个行政区内重要绿地沿着现有路段连接起来，并强化沿途景观植被，以方便各区居民休闲骑行。

其次，规划6条长途绿廊（见"长途绿廊"，P153），将外围绿地与市中心绿地串联在一起，形成通往市区的休闲骑行道路，骑行者途中亦可在公园绿地进行小憩。

最后，沿着市区内的苏州河及黄浦江，设计两条滨水骑行线路（见"滨水骑行路线"，P154），骑行者可边骑行边观赏沿岸风景。

通过以上三种不同路线的叠加，我们获得了绿廊系统规划图（见"完整绿廊系统"，P155）。此套系统将市区内碎片化的绿地连接成一体，不仅可以提升骑行者的骑行体验，同时也强化了市区内公共绿地的连续性。

绿廊系统
Green Cycling Routes

区域内部自行车绿廊
Internal green cycling routes

—— 绿色骑行道 Green cycling routes
■ 主要绿地 Primary green space
▧ 绿地 Green space

0　1 km

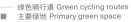
绿色骑行道 Green cycling routes
主要绿地 Primary green space
绿地 Green space

0   1 km

系统规划   153

滨水骑行路线
Riverside cycling routes

——— 绿色骑行道 Green cycling routes
■ 主要绿地 Primary green space
■ 绿地 Green space

0 __ 1 km

完整绿廊系统
Complete green cycling network

───── 绿色骑行道 Green cycling routes
■ 主要绿地 Primary green space
■ 绿地 Green space

0___1 km

系统规划　　　　155

Commuting System

Through the case studies, we found that it is quite common to link the city hubs/public centers to create commuting cycling system. However, due to cultural difference, the definition of public center varies according to different cities.

In Vienna, cultural venues and important historical buildings have basically formed the city's public center, along which the most important cycle lane was planned. In Paris, besides the cultural sites and historic buildings, squares, parks and subway stations are also classified as public centers, and the bicycle commuting system links these spots together. Considering the uniqueness of Shanghai (compared to European cities, Shanghai has larger population and is lack of large public plazas as well as historical and cultural landmarks), we used the cycling system planning in Dublin as a reference, which means to define the area with highest population density as the public center, and to design the routes based on that.

By referring to the *Shanghai Central City District Planning (2004–2020), Understanding Urban Spatial Structure of Shanghai Central City Based on Mobile Phone Data* and onsite investigations, we can be sure that the

通勤系统

通过案例研究我们发现，在样本城市，通过连接城市公共中心来形成网状自行车通勤系统的做法非常普遍。但是由于各城市文化背景的差异，对于公共中心，不同城市有着不同的定义。

在维也纳，文化场所及重要历史建筑基本构成了城市的公共中心，它们由最主要的自行车通勤道串联起来。而在巴黎，除去文化场所和历史建筑，广场、公园及地铁站也属于公共中心，自行车通勤系统将这些点也联系在一起。

考虑到上海城市本身的特殊性（相对欧洲城市缺乏公共广场，缺乏地标性历史文化建筑，人口密度较高），我们更多地借鉴了都柏林的骑行系统规划思路，即将人口活动密度最高的区域定为公共中心，并据此进行路线设计。

area of the highest density in public activities basically equals commercial centers.[2,3]

Then we marked these business centers on the map based on the information from different resources, and divided them into two categories – municipal centers and district-level centers. Each of them are connected to each other with the shortest routes. These two layers were combined together and formed a commuting cycling routes that connect all public centers (commercial centers) in Shanghai. Through this system, the citizens can commute in a more efficient way (see "Commercial Centers", p. 160, "Commuting System (City Level)", p. 161, "Commuting System (District Level)", p. 162 and "Complete Commuting System", p. 163).

根据《上海市中心城分区规划（2004–2020）》《基于手机数据识别上海中心城的城市空间结构》及现场勘查，可以判定，上海中心城区人口活动密度最高的区域基本等同于商业中心。[2, 3]

随后，我们依据各方资料将这些商业中心在地图上标示出来，按市级中心及区级中心分为两类，并沿最短路径将其两两相连。市级及区级的两层网络经过叠加，最终形成了连接上海各公共中心（商业中心）的自行车通勤系统。沿着这套系统，市民可以骑车在中心城区内便捷地穿行[见"商业中心""通勤路线（市级）""通勤路线（区级）""完整通勤路线"，P160–P163]。

2 Wang Jun. A View of Shanghai: To Understand the Spatial Structure of Urban Shanghai through Cellphone Big Data. *The Paper*, http://www.thepaper.cn/newsDetail_forward_1295987, 2015-01-20/2017-07-14.

3 Jiang Lijun. Shanghai metro lines are fully loaded in peak time with 2.5 people per square meter in major stations, http://www.thepaper.cn/baidu.jsp?contid=1354609, 2015-07-20/2017-7-14.

2 王昀. 看上海：用手机大数据看上海城市空间结构[N/OL]. 澎湃，[2015-01-20/2017-07-14]. http://www.thepaper.cn/newsDetail_forward_1295987.

3 姜丽钧. 上海地铁高峰时列车普遍满载，大客流车站每平方米2.5个人[N/OL]. [2015-07-20/2017-7-14]. http://www.thepaper.cn/baidu.jsp?contid=1354609.

通勤系统
Commuting System

商业中心
Commercial centers

■ 办公建筑 Office building
■ 商业建筑 Business building

0＿＿1 km

—— 通勤自行车道（市级）Commuting cycle routes (city level)
■ 办公建筑 Office building
■ 商业建筑 Business building

0 __ 1 km

通勤路线(区级)
Commuting system (district level)

------- 地区级自行车道 Commuting cycle routes (district level)
■ 办公建筑 Office building
■ 商业建筑 Business building

0 __ 1 km

System Planning   162

—— 通勤自行车道（市级）Commuting cycle routes (city level)
----- 地区级自行车道 Commuting cycle routes (district level)
■ 办公建筑 Office building
■ 商业建筑 Business building

0   1 km

"Last Kilometer" System

Since the opening of the first rail transit in Shanghai in 1993, the number of passengers has increased every year, and its trip ratio has exceeded bus transportation for the first time in 2014. According to the *Shanghai City Master Plan (2016－2040)*, the rate of traveling by public transit will take more than half by that time, and rail transit will become the core of public transportation.[4]

The development is in the right direction, yet it is obvious that Shanghai's rail transit has its own congenital defects.

The downtown area is very large, but the transport stations are not evenly located. If we set the service radius as 500 meters, the area beyond the coverage of rail transit will take as high as 57.8% in the city center.

During the process of urban development, due to different economic conditions and population density, each city is somehow effected by the "last kilometer" issue, and Shanghai has comparatively suffered the most. The population density of central Paris is very close to the city center of Shanghai. If we remove the two large public green lands in the east and the west of Paris, the coverage ratio of rail transit reaches 90%, which

最后一公里系统

自1993年上海第一条轨道交通线路开通以来，轨道交通客运量逐年增加，2014年出行比例首次超过了地面公交。根据《上海市城市总体规划2016-2040》，届时上海的公共交通出行率将占一半以上，并且形成以轨道交通为核心的出行结构。[4]

尽管发展方向值得肯定，但我们经研究发现，上海轨交系统的先天缺陷也较为明显。

上海市区面积大，站点分布不均匀。假设以服务半径500 m计算，仅在中心城区内，轨道交通未能覆盖的区域就高达57.8%。

事实上，由于经济状况不同和人口密度的差异，世界各城市均有不同程度的"最后一公里"现象，但相较之下，上海"最后一公里"问题较为严重。通过与国外案例城市的比较，研究发现，中心城区人口密度与上海近似的巴黎，倘若除去城区东西两块大型

4　上海市城市规划设计研究院. 上海市城市总体规划2016-2040 [EB/OL]. [2016-08/2017-07-14] http://www.supdri.com/2040/public/images/gongshi/3.pdf.

4　Shanghai Urban Planning and Design Research Institute. *Shanghai City Master Plan (2016-2040)*. http://www.supdri.com/2040/public/images/gongshi/3.pdf, 2016-08/2017-07-14.

is a very ideal number; even Berlin, a city that only has half the population of Shanghai, has 70% coverage of rail transit in the city center.

The low accessibility to rail station and the super high density of population in the central areas in Shanghai make nearly half of the Shanghai citizens experience low travelling convenience, which is called the "Last Kilometer" issue (see "Paris Metro System and Service Area", p. 168 and "Berlin Rail System and Srvice Area", p. 169).

Although the current statistics shows that bus-to-rail connections account for 2/3 of the combined travel volume (regardless of walking),[5] the ever-changing timetables and increasingly congested ground transport make it less efficient and less convenient for people to travel. Considering the high flexibility of the bike itself and the great potential of the bike-subway combined travel mode (it is proved by the large number of shared bicycles around the metro stations after peak hours in the morning), we conducted the analysis and planning of the "Last Kilometer" areas, proposing a cycling system target on this issue which can help citizens cycle quickly to the metro station.

公共绿地，其轨交覆盖率达90%。而柏林这座人口密度仅为上海一半的城市，尽管其轨交系统覆盖率相对较低，但在中心城区也已达到70%（见"巴黎地铁系统及其服务半径"，P168、"柏林轨交系统及其服务半径"，P169）。

　　轨交站较低的可达性，中心城区极高的人口密度，给上海中心城区近一半的市民出行带来不便，并造成"最后一公里"问题。

　　尽管现有数据表明，"公共汽车－轨交"的接驳方式占组合出行量的2/3(不考虑步行)[5]，然而，不确定的时刻表以及愈发拥堵的地面交通，使得此类组合出行效率偏低，时间成本过高，市民出行依旧不够便利。考虑到自行车本身的机动性以及"自行车－地铁"组合出行的巨大潜力（早高峰后地铁站附近大量出现的共享单车也验证了这一点），我们针对这一出行需求，对"最后一公里"区域进行分析及规划设计。希望规划出的"最后一公里"网络能为市民出行提供另外种可能，使他们可以通过骑行快速抵达轨交站点。

5　姚瑶. 上海市轨道交通换乘接驳相关问题研究[J].
交通与运输，2016 (12): 56.

巴黎地铁系统及其服务半径
Paris Metro System and Service Area

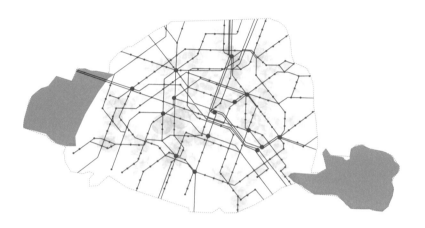

服务半径 Service area
● 地铁站点 Metro station
—— 地铁线 Metro line

0   1 km

柏林轨交系统及其服务半径
Berlin Rail System and Srvice Area

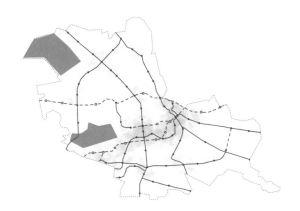

—— 建成地铁线路 Completed metro line
---- 规划地铁线路 Planned metro line
• 建成地铁站及服务半径 Completed metro station and service area
∘ 规划地铁站及服务半径 Planned metro station and service area
■ 主要绿地 Primary green space

0 ___ 1 km

系统规划 　　　　　　169

Sphere of Influence

We need to find out the specific location and scope of the "Last Kilometer" before planning. According to *Shanghai Rail Transit 2020*,[6] we marked out the subway lines and stations in the city center (see "Shanghai Current Metro System", p. 172) and located the service areas by drawing a 500 meter radius around each subway station (see "Metro Station and Service Area", p. 173), leaving the uncovered area as the scope of the "Last Kilometer". After estimation, we found out that it happens in all city centers in Shanghai, covering all together 167 km², which is 57.8% of the area of the central city. This problem affects 3.42 million people, accounting for 55% of the citizens in the city center. Therefore, it is obvious to identify the "Last Kilometer" as a big problem in terms of the scope of area and population it affected (see "The 'Last Kilometer' Area", p. 174).

Later, the team further refined the map, coloring different programs on the map, such as schools, offices, residence... etc. Based on the final results, we found that the "Last Kilometer" covers various programs. In other words, all kinds of people, no matter they are workers, teachers, ordinary office workers, or students, will be somehow disturbed by this issue. It is a national problem that we all will face (see "Programs in the 'Last Kilometer' Area", p. 175).

影响范围

在规划前，首先要找出上海中心城区"最后一公里"的具体位置及范围。我们根据《上海市轨道交通规划2020》[6]画出了中心城区中的地铁线路与站点（见"上海现有轨交系统"，P172），并以地铁站为圆心，以500 m为半径找出站点服务区域（见"地铁站及服务范围"，P173），其中未覆盖的区域即"最后一公里"区域。经估算后发现，调查的上海中心城区均有此问题。调查区域总面积为167 km²，占中心城区的57.8%，影响人数342万人，为中心城区户籍人口的55%。由此可见，在市中心范围内，"最后一公里"出行难都是一个大问题（见"'最后一公里'区域"，P174）。

随后，我们通过颜色将不同功能进行区分，如学校、办公、住宅区、工业区等。根据最终结果可见，"最后一公里"区域涵盖了各类功能（见"'最后一公里'区域功能"，P175）。

Shanghai Metro. A Big Year of Metro Construction! 10 Rails of 216 Miles to be Constructed. http://www.shmetro.com/ node49/201603/con114609.htm, 2016-03-03 / 2017-07-14.

6　上海地铁. 地铁建设大年来了！10条线路216公里全面开建[EB/OL]. [2016-03-03/2017-07-14] http://www.shmetro.com/node49/201603/ con114609.htm.

上海现有轨交系统
Shanghai current metro system

── 地铁线 Metro line

0 ___ 1 km

地铁站 Metro station
服务半径 Service area

0 ___ 1 km

系统规划 173

地铁站 Metro station
未服务区域 Unserved area

0___1 km

· 　地铁站 Metro station
■ 　工业区 Industrial area
■ 　工作区 Office area
　　住宅区 Residential area
　　学校 School

0　　1 km

To find out the specific number of people who are affected by the "Last Kilometer" problem near each metro station, we divided the jurisdictional area of each station with the Tyson polygon (see "Jurisdictional Area of Metro Station", p. 178), then calculated the effect number of people within each jurisdictional area according to the population density of each district except airports, large-scale industrial part and large green lands, and marked them out by different tones of colors (see "Programs in Jurisdictional Area", p. 179). Areas marked in darkest color are most seriously affected (see "Population in Jurisdictional Area", p. 180). Based on our estimation, the area in Kangning Road Station and Guangyue Road Station of the planning has more than one hundred thousand people affected by the "Last Kilometer" issue, and most areas have more than ten thousand affected people. The planning cannot solve all the problems at the same time, so we picked the middle number – 25,000 as the dividing line, and focused on improving the cycling condition in the areas over this number (see "'The Last Kilometer' Key Area", p. 181).

也就是说，不论是工人、上班族，还是学生，各类人群或多或少都会碰到出行困难的问题，此问题也是一个全民问题。

　　而为了找出每个轨交站附近受"最后一公里"问题困扰的具体人数（见"地铁站管辖区域"，P178），我们利用泰森多边形划分出各轨交站管辖区域(见"管辖区域功能"，P179)，并配合先前的图纸，在除去机场、大型工业区、大型绿地后根据各区人口密度估算出各轨交站管辖区内受影响的人数，并通过颜色深浅进行区分（见"管辖区人口数量"，P180）。图中颜色最深的部分即"最后一公里"问题最为严重的区域。根据估算，规划中的康宁路站与广粤路站区域内受"最后一公里"影响的人数均超过了10万人，而大部分区域受影响人数过万。考虑到规划落实过程中无法同时解决所有问题，因此，以受影响人数中间段25 000人为分界线，重点考虑改善这些区域内的骑行系统（见"'最后一公里'重点区域"，P181）。

地铁站管辖区域
Jurisdictional area of metro station

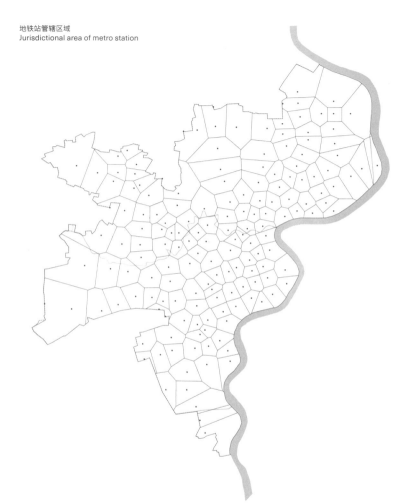

· 　地铁站 Metro station

0　　1 km

管辖区域功能
Programs in jurisdictional area

- 地铁站 Metro station
- ■ 工业区 Industrial area
- ■ 工作区 Office area
- 住宅区 Residential area
- 学校 School

0___1 km

管辖区人口数量
Population in jurisdictional area

- 0–10 000人 people
- 10 000–25 000人 people
- 25 000–45 000人 people
- 45 000–75 000人 people
- 75 000+人 people
- 工业区边界 Industrial area boundary

0 __ 1 km

"最后一公里"重点区域
The "Last Kilometer" key area

0–10 000人 people
10 000–25 000人 people
25 000–45 000人 people
45 000–75 000人 people
75 000+人 people
工业区边界 Industrial area boundary
—— 2.5万人口分界线 25 000 people dividing line

0 __ 1 km

系统规划   181

"Last Kilometer" System Planning

For this large number of people who have problems to access the subway, we planned to connect all main roads within each region to form a network, so that the cyclists who came out the neighborhood can immediately get into the cycling system. Then the network is connected with the main road which leads to the closest subway station (see "'Last Kilometer' System (Part)", pp. 184–185). Through this connection the cyclists can access the subway station in the most rapid way. Through this logic, by planning two layered road, the "Last Kilometer" cycling system is formed (see "'Last Kilometer' System" (Complete), p. 186).

"最后一公里"系统规划

对于这部分出行困难、数量庞大的市民，我们首先规划了区域内的所有组团道路，形成密集网络，使"最后一公里"内骑行者可以从任意点出发后直接进入骑行系统道路网[见"'最后一公里'系统（局部）"，P184-P185]。随后，网络经由主干道接入轨交站，市民可沿此道路骑行抵达站点。遵循这一基本逻辑，规划出这两个层级的道路，"最后一公里"骑行系统得以形成[见"'最后一公里'系统（完整）"，P186]。

"最后一公里"系统（局部）
"Last Kilometer" System (Part)

● 地铁站 Metro station
— 主要骑行道 Primary cycling routes
— 次要骑行道 Branch cycling routes

"最后一公里"系统（完整）
"Last Kilometer" System (Complete)

- 地铁站 Metro station
------- 2.5万人口分界线 Dividing line from 25 000 people
—— 主要骑行道 Primary cycling routes
—— 次要骑行道 Branch cyling routes

0　1 km

上海自行车道网络
Shanghai Cycling Network

- —— 绿道系统 Green cycling network
- —— 通勤系统 Commuting system
- —— 最后一公里 "Last kilometer" system
- —— 绿道+商圈系统 Green cycling + commuting system
- —— 绿道+最后一公里系统 Green cycling + "last kilometer" system
- —— 商圈+最后一公里系统 Commuting system + "last kilometer" system
- ⬚ 样本基地 Sample site

0   1 km

"Fan" Structure

Green corridor system, commute route system, the "Last Kilometer" system added up to a central cycling system in Shanghai, which is also a basic structure of our concept (see "Shanghai Cycling Network", p. 187). Due to the unexpected urban expansion and the future of slow traffic development, the cycling network will be further divided or modified based on this structure. Unlike other bicycle-friendly cities, Shanghai has its unique cycling system with higher density at the end due to the "Last Kilometer" issue. To understand the nature of the entire cycling system, we distinguished each layer with CMYK color system (C for "Last Kilometer", M for commuting, Y for the green corridor). The original colors, plus the new color after the combining of two original colors, for example, green and purple, helped us to understand the specific nature of each route system as well as the cycling system in general after being overlapped together. Through the final map of the overlaid system, we will find out that the unique "Last Kilometer" issue in Shanghai – the entire system is in a "fan" structure with higher density at both ends. Each layer has its own characters while maintain certain similarities. The "Last Kilometer" issue is located on the outer ring; the commercial commuting system is in the city

扇形架构

绿廊系统、通勤系统、"最后一公里"系统，这三层系统的叠加完成了上海中心城区自行车系统近阶段的构想，这也是最基本的骨架构想（见"上海自行车道网络"，P187）。由于城市发展的不可预料性以及慢行系统发展的趋势，未来上海的骑行网络会在此基础上作进一步细分或调整。而与其他自行车友好城市案例的骑行规划不同，由于上海本地的"最后一公里"问题，规划的骑行系统越到尾端反而越密集，形成了其独特的骑行网络。为了厘清整个骑行系统的性质，我们利用潘通色对不同规划层进行上色（"最后一公里"–蓝色，商业–粉色，绿廊–黄色）。其原色及两两叠加后形成的新颜色（绿色，紫色）有助于了解每条系统道路的具体属性及叠加后骑行系统的整体特征。通过最终的系统叠加图可以看到，由于上海特有的"最后一公里"问题，整个系统呈扇

center, and the green corridor system is running in between. Based on such character of the cycling system, we abstracted a sample area and developed the design. It is based on Yan'an Elevated Road and started from Hongqiao Airport, following the Suzhou River down to the bank of the Huangpu River. According to the nature of the cycling lane, this section not only acquires the characters of other layers, but also includes the major landscape belts in Shanghai. We also picked out different plots within this section to cover as many as possible activities to represent the new urban look after the improvement of the cycling system. Among this sample slice, we selected different sites which not only cover wide range of activities, but also show the cycling system can improve the urban images.

状，尾端比较密集。其中，每个分支特征都较为明显且具有相似性，即外围"最后一公里"，市中心为商业通勤系统，其间穿插着绿廊系统。基于该骑行系统的特性，我们截取了其中一支较有代表性的样本片段并深入节点进行具体设计。这一切片基于延安路高架，从虹桥机场开始，顺着苏州河一直延伸到黄浦江边。从骑行道路性质上来看，此片段不但具备其他分支的特征，同时也涉及上海最主要的景观带。而在具体节点选择上，团队也挑选了不同地块，以涵盖多样的人群活动，并展现骑行系统改善后所能带来的新的城市风貌。

设计愿景｜骑行上海
Design Vision:
Cycling@Shanghai

Pinghe Community, Xijiao State Guest Hotel, Jing'an Temple Metro Station... These sample sites are either typical, or important nodes of the city. For the cycling system in these area, the team proposed different strategies, which may seem idealistic today, but they are still constructive in the long term. Besides, we select some typical roads, eg, West Hailun Road, Gonghexin Road as design samplets and give improvement suggestions.

平和公寓、西郊宾馆、静安寺地铁站……这些样本基地，或具有普遍性，或属于城市重要节点。针对这些区域，我们所提出的解决策略在今日看来可能略为理想化，但从长远看依然具有一定的建设性。此外针对一些典型样本路段，如海伦西路、共和新路，我们也给出了一些改善建议。

Pinghe Community

Pinghe Community is in the rim of the "Last Kilometer" area, and the community is surrounded by branch roads with no division between cycling routes and vehicles routes. In the peak hours, vehicles and non-motor vehicles will cross the routes of each other and will cause traffic flow inefficiency. It also brings security risks to the cyclists, and the cycling experience is quite bad (see "Pinghe Community before", p. 200).

In order to solve this chaotic situation, and to allow the cyclists enjoy a safer cycling environment, we designed a hedge between the vehicle route and cycling route to isolate and to prevent the two flows interfere with each other. In addition, the hedge can also reduce the noise and tail gas of motor vehicles, enhancing the cycling experience (see "Pinghe Community after", p. 201).

平和公寓

平和公寓是位于"最后一公里"区域内的终端小区，小区周围道路为城市支路，没有机非隔离设施，仅以划线区分（见"平和公寓改造前"，P200）。在高峰时段，机动车与非机动车相互占道，导致通行效率低下，同时也产生巨大的安全隐患，骑行体验十分糟糕。

　　为了解决这一混乱的状况，使骑行者一出小区就能进入安全的骑行环境，设计通过绿篱对机动车道与非机动车道进行隔离，以防止机非相互干扰。此外，绿篱也能减少机动车噪声与尾气，提升骑行体验（见"平和公寓改造后"，P201）。

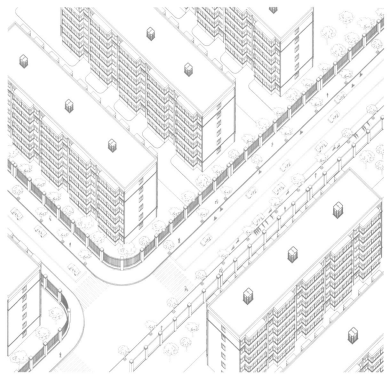

平和公寓改造前
Pinghe Community before

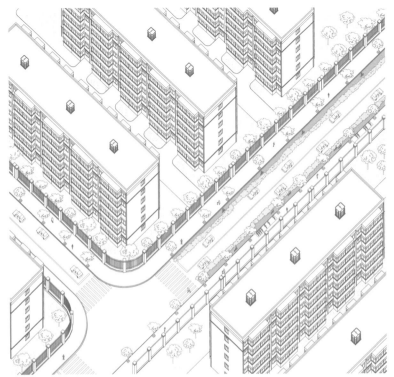

平和公寓改造后
Pinghe Community after

Xijiao State Guest Hotel

Xijiao State Guest Hotel is an important pilot of the green corridor system. It sits next to a residential neighborhood and surrounded by large areas of lake and green land. However, the green land is enclosed from the public with walls, cyclists and passengers cannot enjoy this natural landscape from outside (see "Xijiao State Guest Hotel before", p. 206).

The design aims to give the unused and precious green land back to the public. We opened the enclosing wall between Longxi Road and the hotel, introducing the bicycle route into the green land. When cycling along the road, the cyclists can enjoy the view along the route while staying away from the bustling motor vehicles (see "Xijiao State Guest Hotel after", p. 207).

西郊宾馆

西郊宾馆为绿廊系统的一个重要节点，其附近为住宅区，宾馆周边环绕着大片湖面及绿地（见"西郊宾馆改造前"，P206）。然而这片绿地对外封闭，四周均以围墙进行隔离，经过这一区域的骑行者和行人无法享受到这片自然景观。

　　设计旨在将目前闲置但又宝贵的绿地资源开放给公众。我们将龙溪路与西郊宾馆间的围墙完全打开，并将骑行道引入绿地。骑行者在避免机动车干扰的同时，还能欣赏沿途的景色，并在长椅上略作休憩（见"西郊宾馆改造后"，P207）。

西郊宾馆改造前
Xijiao State Guest Hotel before

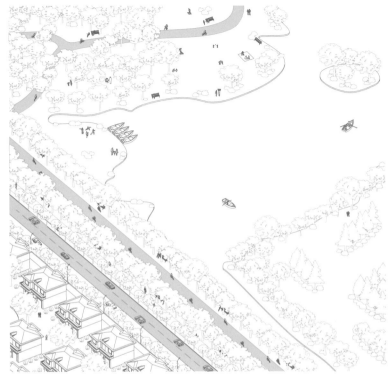

西郊宾馆改造后
Xijiao State Guest Hotel after

Beixinjing Metro Station

Beixinjing Metro Station is also in the area of the "Last Kilometer". Large bicycle parking area is needed at the entrance plaza, but there is no planning to clarify the parking infrastructure, leaving the parking in disorder. Besides, there's only one entrance for the plaza and the cycle lane that is hundreds of meters long, which brings great difficulties for the cyclists. The general quality of this public space is bad, which is also partly caused by the vehicle parking on the pedestrian street (see "Beixinjing Subway Station before", p. 212).

We proposed to use a hedge to separate the cycle lane and the vehicle lane. The hedge will reduce the noise and pollution from four two-way motor lanes. Besides, a cycle parking area is set for the cyclists, and multiple exits are planned in the entrance plaza as well as the motor vehicle route to make it more convenient for the cyclist to ride and stop. Motor vehicles are forbidden to enter the plaza to improve the quality of the public space in general (see "Beixinjing Subway Station after", p. 213).

北新泾地铁站

北新泾地铁站是"最后一公里"问题区域内的地铁站，其入口广场处自行车停放需求很大，但缺乏明确的停车设施规划，乱停放现象明显。此外，长达几百米的非机动车道与入口广场只有一个出入口，给骑行者即骑即停带来不便。此公共空间整体品质较差，与人行道上大量停放的机动车也有关（见"北新泾地铁站改造前"，P212）。

　　针对这一节点，设计首先通过绿篱进行机非隔离，减少双向8车道对骑行者的影响。并沿街建立专用的停车设施，明确停车区域。在入口广场与机动车道间加设多个出入口，以方便骑行者即骑即停。为了提升整体公共空间品质，禁止机动车侵入步行广场（见"北新泾地铁站改造后"，P213）。

北新泾地铁站改造前
Beixinjing Subway Station before

北新泾地铁站改造后
Beixinjing Subway Station after

Intersection of Yan'an Elevated Road

This spot is located at the intersection of Kaixuan Road and West Yan'an Road. The east-west Yan'an Road is a main road in Shanghai that consists of 12 lanes. Currently cycling is forbidden, but there are still a lot of cyclists passing through and occupying the motorways and the pedestrian street. For the cyclists, the biggest problem is the long-time waiting for the green traffic light. Sometimes it takes 3 minutes to wait for 2 times just for turning left (see Yan'an Elevated Road before", p. 218).

As a commuting route that connects the "Last Kilometer" area and the city center, a comfortable and continuous cycling experience matters most. Since the south side of the street has more green space and sun light, we planned a two-way cycle lane here, and expand it based on the existing pedestrian bridge. Then the cyclists can avoid the red light and enter the bridge directly with the cycling ramp (see Yan'an Elevated Road after", p. 219).

延安路高架快速路交叉路口

此节点位于延安西路凯旋路交叉口，东西向延安路为12车道的城市主干路。目前延安西路属于非机动车禁行路段，但是仍有较多非机动车占用机动车道或人行道骑行（见"延安路高架快速路交叉路口改造前"，P218）。对于骑行者来说，大路口问题在于红灯等待时间太长，若要左转，有时需要等待两个红灯，长达3分钟。

作为连接"最后一公里"和市中心的快速路，长途骑行的舒适度和骑行连贯性是关键点。考虑到南侧绿地景观居多，且有长时间日照，我们在此添加了双向自行车道，并且利用原有的人行天桥，进行拓宽加建，使得骑行者可以避开红灯等候，通过自行车坡道直接上天桥（见"延安路高架快速路交叉路口改造后"，P219）。

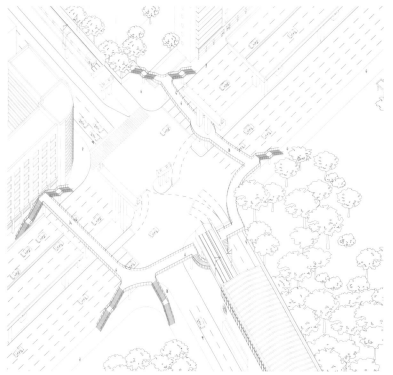

延安路高架快速路交叉路口改造前
Yan'an Elevated Road before

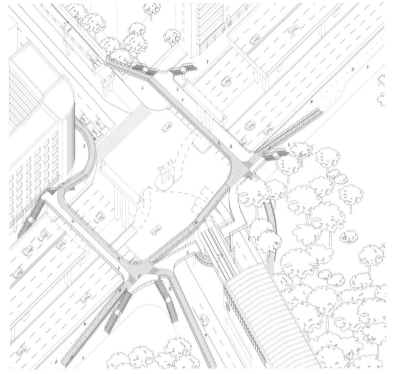

延安路高架快速路交叉路口改造后
Yan'an Elevated Road after

Jing'an Temple Metro Station Line 7

Jing'an Temple station is located along the elevated way of Milddle Yan'an Road, surrounded by commercial centers, parks and culture attractions. The traffic flow is very large, but cycling is banned below the elevated road. There are limited cycle parking spaces in front of the metro station, so most of the bikes are parked under the elevated road. Due to the limited parking space underneath, cyclists have to cross a three-way motorway to park their bike, which is very inconvenient (see "Jing'an Temple Station of Metro Line 7 before", p. 224).

We proposed to insert a cycling lane in the Middle Yan'an Road and fully use the space under the elevated road. Two parking areas are planned to be merged into one, and a multi-layered parking ramp is planned to enable the cyclists to ride all the way to the elevated space and park their bicycles (see "Jing'an Temple Station of Metro Line 7 after", p. 225).

7号线静安寺地铁站

7号线静安寺地铁站紧靠延安中路高架，周围有商业中心，公园与人文景点，往来人流量非常大，但高架下方自行车禁行。静安寺地铁站口停车空间有限，目前大部分自行车停在相邻的延安中路高架下方。由于近地铁口处高架下停车空间不足，使得人们需要经过一段三机动车道的马路去另一片区域停车，增加了停车路程（见"7号线静安寺地铁站改造前"，P224）。

设计考虑开放延安中路作为骑行道路，并充分利用高架下方的垂直空间，将两侧停车点并为一处，修建多层的停车设施并用坡道连接上方空间，使得骑行者可以较为连续地骑行至就近点完成停车（见"7号线静安寺地铁站改造后"，P225）。

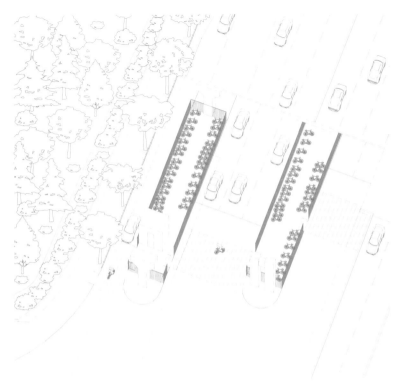

7号线静安寺地铁站改造前
Jing'an Temple Station of Metro Line 7 before

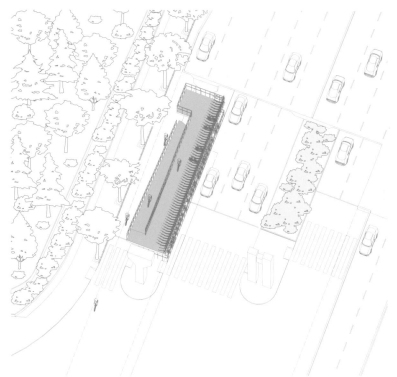

7号线静安寺地铁站改造后
Jing'an Temple Station of Metro Line 7 after

IAPM Shopping Mall

IAPM Shopping-mall is located in the CBD of Huaihai Road and South Shanxi Road. There is a huge flow along the roads. However, cycling is banned at the Middle Huaihai Road, and there's no cycle parking facilities planned around the shopping mall. People cannot go to the shopping by bike (see "Huanmao IAPM Shopping-mall before", p. 230).

We proposed a two-way bike lane close to the shopping mall, which is a bit lifted to be isolated from the motorway. At the same time, considering the high value of the area, we plan to apply the Japan Eco-cycle underground parking system that has smaller footprint and simpler appearance, to provide enough parking space for the cyclists (see "Huanmao IAPM Shopping-mall after", p. 231).

环贸IAPM商场

环贸IAPM商场位于淮海中路陕西南路商业区，人流量很大，但是淮海中路自行车禁行，规划时商场沿主街也并没有考虑到自行车交通问题或设立自行车停车位，骑行前来消费，多有不便（见"环贸IAPM商场改造前"，P230）。

　　设计考虑此处机动车限速，在靠近IAPM一侧铺设双向自行车道，仅通过地坪抬高与机动车道隔离。考虑到此处寸土寸金，所以可采用日本Eco-cycle地下停车系统，占地面积小，外形简洁，可为骑行者提供便捷的停车服务（见"环贸IAPM商场改造后"，P231）。

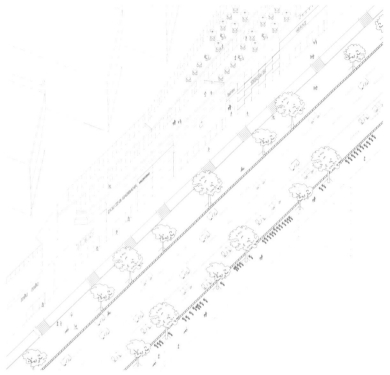

环贸IAPM商场改造前
Huanmao IAPM Shopping-mall before

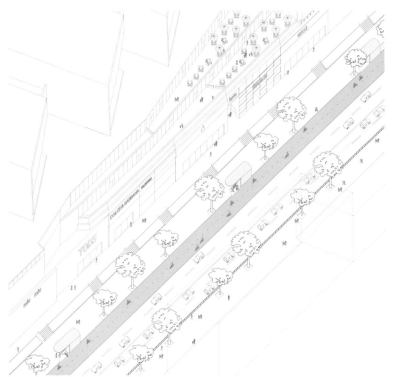

环贸IAPM商场改造后
Huanmao IAPM Shopping-mall after

North-South Elevated Road

The North Chengdu Road system was divided by the Suzhou River. People can cross the river with 4 pedestrian staircases with no cycling facilities. Cyclists can only pass the river by Xinzha Bridge (250 m away from North Chengdu Road), which has greatly affected the continuity of cycling (see "North-South Elevated Road before", p. 236).

Our design tries to extend the four staircases into a cycling ramp, which will be separated by green spaces from the other 12 routes. Then cyclists and pedestrians can enjoy the view of Suzhou River from the bridge (see "North-South Elevated Road after", p. 237).

南北过河高架

成都北路被苏州河分隔，现有人行过河设施为4个步行楼梯，利用率较低，并没有骑行设施，自行车只能通过旁边的新闸桥（距离250 m）过河，严重影响了骑行的连续性（见"南北过河高架改造前"，P236）。

设计将4个步行楼梯拓展为自行车骑行坡道，并通过绿植将桥面上的慢行系统与其他12条车道隔离。如此，骑行者与行人可以在桥上观赏苏州河风景（见"南北过河高架改造后"，P237）。

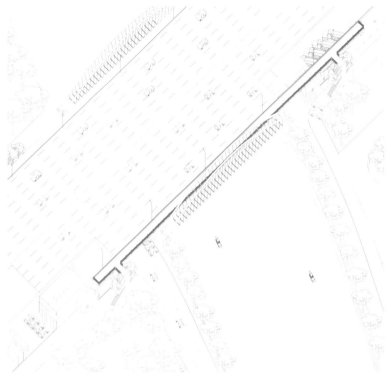

南北过河高架改造前
North-South Elevated Road before

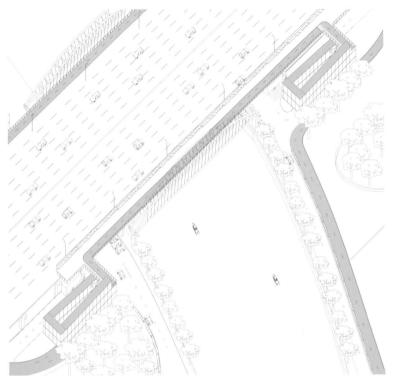

南北过河高架改造后
North-South Elevated Road after

Green Cycle Route along Suzhou River

In the green cycle route system, Waibaidu Bridge is the intersection of Huangpu River green cycle route and Suzhou River green cycle route. Multiple historical buildings and culture attractions are located around this area, such as the Rock Bund, the Union Church, Shanghai Tower, among many others. As the main attraction in Shanghai, Suzhou River has no cycle lane, tourists can only view the river either through walking or driving, which limit the possibilities of exploring Suzhou River (see "Suzhou River landscape greenway before", p. 242).

Therefore, we planned a green cycle route and cycle parking area along the Suzhou River, so tourists can view this attraction either by walking or cycling. Considering there are limited angles of taking pictures, people can barely see the complete elevation of the bridge, thus we introduced a dock in our design, guiding the tourists to watch the Waibaidu Bridge from a new perspective, providing a new spot for the tourists to take selfies (see "Suzhou River landscape greenway after", p. 243).

苏州河景观绿道

外白渡桥是绿地系统中滨江绿道与苏州河绿道的交点，周边文化景点众多，外滩源、新天安堂、上海大厦等，都是上海历史变迁的见证。苏州河作为上海市重要景观，沿河却没有设置专门的自行车道，使得人们只能步行或乘车，很大程度上限制了参观的自由性（见"苏州河景观绿道改造前"，P242）。

因此，设计首先在沿岸的道路中开辟出专门的自行车绿道与自行车停放点，让游客既能步行参观，又能骑行游览。考虑到外白渡桥这一历史建筑取景角度有限，在过去影视作品中几乎没有完整的立面形象，因此在设计时，特地加设一个临水观景平台，引导人们从另一个角度观赏外白渡桥，也为热爱自拍的游客提供了一个新的取景点（见"苏州河景观绿道改造后"，P243）。

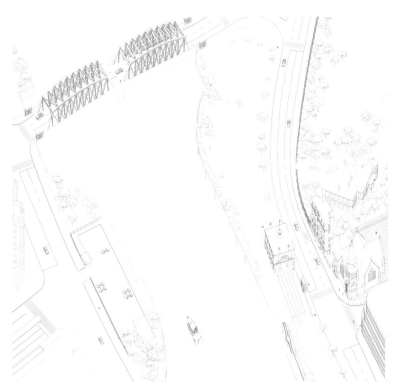

苏州河景观绿道改造前
Suzhou River landscape greenway before

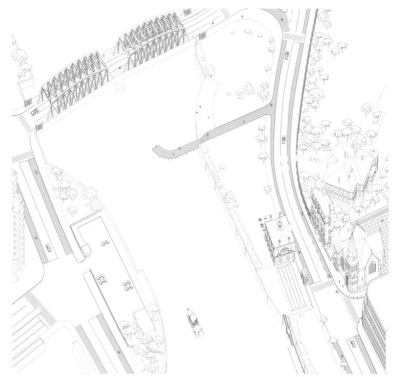

苏州河景观绿道改造后
Suzhou River landscape greenway after

Shiliupu Dock

The Shiliupu Dock is an important traffic hub for walking and cycling from Puxi to Pudong. On the existing Shiliupu Dock, the bicycle parking area is very far away from the dock, and the cyclists need to park their bicycle first and get on the boat after walking a few hundred meters. Cyclist who try to cross the river with their bicycles will have to ride together with the pedestrians on the ramp to the dock, which will be very dangerous (see Shiliupu Dock before, p. 248).

We hope to move the parking area as close as possible to the dock, so we transformed the pillars on the dock into parking railings, allowing the cyclists to transfer to the boat immediately after parking the bicycles. Meanwhile, the two ramps connecting the dock are planned to be divided into routes for bikes and for pedestrians to avoid conflicts (see Shiliupu Dock after, p. 249).

十六铺码头

十六铺码头是从浦西到浦东步行和骑行的重要交通节点。此处现有的自行车停放点距离码头过远，骑行者停完车后需步行几百米上船；而对带车过江的骑行者而言，在通往码头坡道上的步行人群中骑行，存在安全隐患（见"十六铺码头改造前"，P248）。

改造希望停车点尽可能接近码头，于是将原本码头上的柱子改成停车栏杆，使得骑行者停完车转乘渡轮更为便利。同时将连接码头的两条坡道划分成自行车专用道与步行专用道，以避免流线混乱（见"十六铺码头改造后"，P249）。

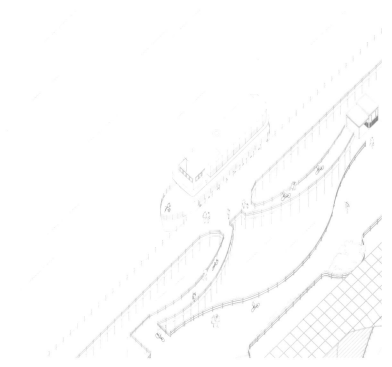

十六铺码头改造前
Shiliupu Dock before

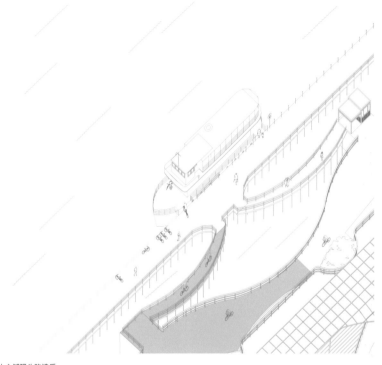

十六铺码头改造后
Shiliupu Dock after

设计愿景 249

Old Dock Area along Huangpu River

The original warehouses have been converted into cafes and restaurants in the old dock area along Huangpu River. However, the best landscape area along the river was designed as a belt parking area, which is very inefficiently used and has blocked the view of the waterscape (see "Huangpu River Old Dock before", p. 254).

In our proposal, we hope to open the view of the river as much as possible, so we planned to transform the parking area into a beach that combines cycling, relaxation and entertainment. We also designed a swimming pool of purified river water for people to relax and enjoy the landscape of the city (see "Huangpu River Old Dock after", p. 255).

黄浦江滨江老码头

黄浦江滨江老码头地区，原来的库房已被改造为以咖啡、餐饮功能为主的店铺，然而沿滨江最好的景观区域却被设计成带状停车场，不但使用率不高，还阻隔了人们欣赏江景的视线（见"黄浦江滨江老码头改造前"，P254）。

设计希望尽可能开放江景，将此处停车场改造为一个骑行、休憩、娱乐相结合的沙滩。沿岸处采用隔离堤坝圈出一块净化的江水，用于游泳等水上项目。骑行路过的人可以坐下来喝一杯，在沙滩晒太阳或是下江游泳。此处设计希望给市民提供一个近距离接触自然及观赏都市景观的场所（见"黄浦江滨江老码头改造后"，P255）。

黄浦江滨江老码头改造前
Huangpu River Old Dock before

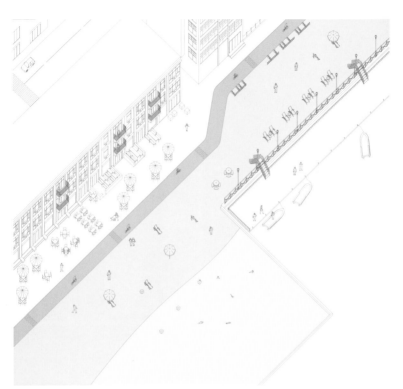

黄浦江滨江老码头改造后
Huangpu River Old Dock after

设计愿景   255

West Hailun Road

It is a east-west one-way road with no separation lines. The ground floor is for commercial use, mainly focus on F&B, and the the the second floor is occupied by lane houses.

West Hailun Road is a shortcut to the Xinjianlu tunnel, so there are a lot of motor vehicles passing through this road, sometimes there are very large trucks. However, due to the limited width of the road itself and the cycle parking space along the road, the current division of road is inconvenient either for the pedestrian or the cyclists (see "West Hailun Road plan and section before", p. 262).

Since the road is close to the residential area and the river, with great landscape value, we would suggest to transform it into a cycle lane, combining the catering along both sides. We also plan to widen one side of the sidewalk to allow stores placing outdoor leisure facilities, creating comfortable street space. Cycle parking will be centralized on parallel street to avoid interruption on the cycling (see "West Hailun Road axonometric", pp. 264–265).

海伦西路

该路段东西走向，为单向道，无划线。一层临街为商业，以餐饮为主，二层以上为里弄住宅。

由于海伦西路是通往新建路隧道的一条捷径，因而有相当多的机动车由此通过，而且不乏各种大型货车。但由于街道本身很窄，两边还需要停放非机动车，现有的路权分配给往来行人和骑行者均带来不便（见"海伦西路平剖图-改造前"，P262）。

由于这条道路紧临住宅区及河道，往来居民较多，景观潜力较好，我们建议将这条路改为自行车专用道，结合两边餐饮功能，规划为慢行街道。设计将一侧人行道加宽，在方便行人行走的同时也可供商户摆放户外休闲设施，营造舒适的街道空间。而非机动车以局部集中、平行于街道的方式停车，以避免存取车时对自行车道造成干扰（见"海伦西路轴测图"，P264-P265）。

海伦西路平剖图–改造前
West Hailun Road plan and section before

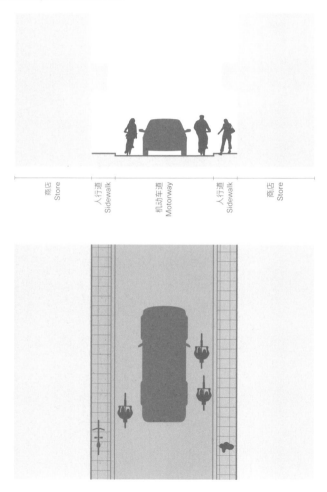

商店 Store　人行道 Sidewalk　机动车道 Motorway　人行道 Sidewalk　商店 Store

海伦西路平剖图–改造后
West Hailun Road plan and section after

商店 Store　　人行道 Sidewalk　　机动车道 Cycle lane　　人行道 Sidewalk　　商店 Store

设计愿景　　　　　263

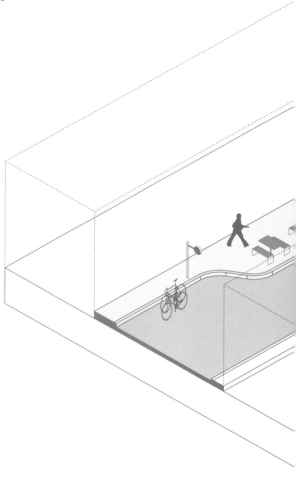

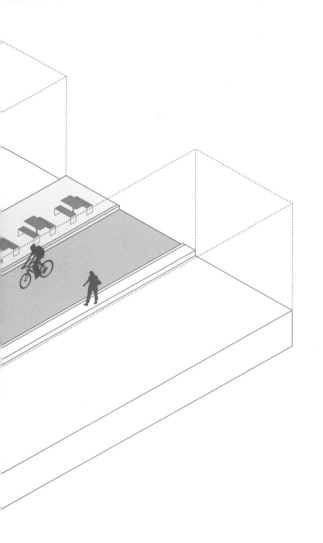

Gonghexin Road (Yanchang Road)

The south-north road is the main road in Zhabei District. There are 6-floor residential buildings along the road. The Yanchang Road section has 11 vehicle routes, including two-way lanes, plus the South-North Elevated Road of 6 lanes above. The 17 lanes in total have brought a lot noise and tail gas pollution. The cycling lane and motor vehicle lane are merely separated by low concrete pier, which makes the cycling experience relatively bad. Also, cyclists have to wait for long for the left turn signal, and many of them choose to turn left directly at the intersection, often blocking other cyclists (see "Gonghexin Road plan and section before", p. 270).

We planned to remove one motor vehicle lane at each side and to transform the one-way cycle lanes in both the east and west side into two-way cycle lanes to simplify the process of turning left and to avoid the vehicles going in the opposite direction. Moreover, we plan to separate the motor vehicles and non-motor vehicles by adding the green belt along the two sides of the cycle lane to provide a shaded and quiet cycling environment for the cyclists (see "Gonghexin Road axonometric", p. 272).

共和新路（延长路段）

该路段南北走向，是闸北区的主干道路。道路两旁为六层居住建筑。延长路段拥有双向共11条机动车道，其上方为6车道的南北高架。上下17车道带来了巨大的噪音及尾气污染，而骑行道与机动车道之间，仅以水泥矮墩隔离。这种隔离方式相较这条超宽道路来说作用微乎其微，因而虽整条道路骑行较为连续，但其整体骑行体验较差。此外，道路的尺度过宽、不同向的车流较多，造成骑行左转信号灯周期长，因此为了便捷，许多人选择在路口直接左转逆向行驶，形成很多安全隐患，也给正常骑行者带来阻碍(见"共和新路平剖图–改造前"，P270)。

我们在道路两侧各取消一条机动车道，将原有东西两面的单向自行车道都修改为双向骑行车道，以简化骑行者左转程序，解决原有的逆行问题。此外，通过在自行车道两旁增加绿化带并植梧桐树来进行机非隔离，骑行者得以拥有一个较安静的绿荫遮蔽的骑行环境（见"共和新路轴测图"，P272–P273）。

共和新路平剖图–改造前
Gonghexin Road plan and section before

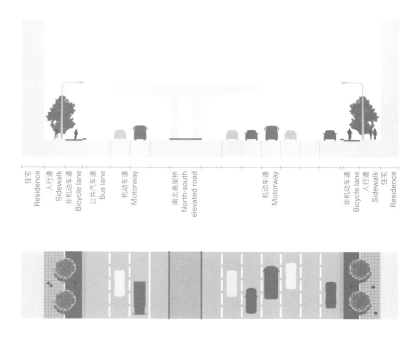

住宅 Residence
人行道 Sidewalk
非机动车道 Bicycle lane
公共汽车道 Bus lane
机动车道 Motorway
南北高架桥 North-south elevated road
机动车道 Motorway
非机动车道 Bicycle lane
人行道 Sidewalk
住宅 Residence

共和新路平剖图-改造后
Gonghexin Road plan and section after

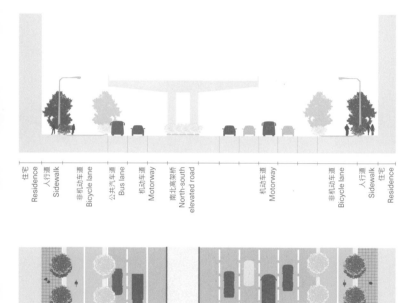

住宅 Residence
人行道 Sidewalk
非机动车道 Bicycle lane
公共汽车道 Bus lane
机动车道 Motorway
南北高架桥 North-south elevated road
机动车道 Motorway
非机动车道 Bicycle lane
人行道 Sidewalk
住宅 Residence

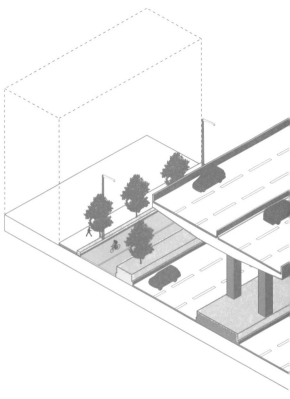

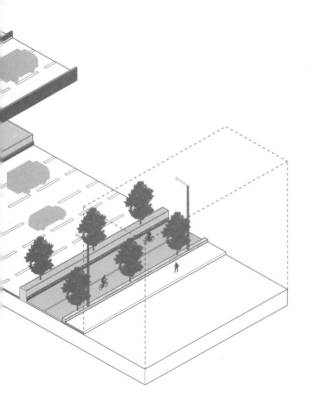

Xinhua Road

It is an east-west and one-way commercial street. There is a bus waiting zone where allows the bus stopping and bicycle parking. The current design did not consider the surrounding circulations. When the cyclists are taking or parking their bicycles near the waiting zone, they will block the cycle lane and the cyclists flow behind (see "Xinhua Road plan and section before", p. 278).

The design cancelled the cycle parking function of the isolation zone, and transferred it into a bus waiting zone. The bicycle parking is moved to the sidewalk, where cyclists can park their bicycles here and avoid interrupting the cyclists flow when picking their bicycles (see "Xinhua Road axonometric", p. 279).

新华路

该路段东西走向，为单向道，道路两侧为临街商业。区域内有一个公交等候岛，供公交停车，也供停放自行车。这一设计的问题在于没有考虑周边流线，骑行者在等候岛附近取车或停车时，会阻挡骑行道，打断后方自行车流（见"新华路平剖图－改造前"，P278）。

我们取消了岛上的停车功能，将其设计为仅供人们等候公交车的站台。自行车的停放被移至人行道，以避免打扰骑行流线（见"新华路轴测图"，P279）。

新华路平剖图-改造前
Xinhua Road plan and section before

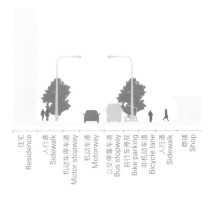

住宅 Residence
人行道 Sidewalk
机动车停车道 Motor stopway
机动车道 Motorway
公交停靠车道 Bus stopway
自行车停放 Bike parking
非机动车道 Bicycle lane
人行道 Sidewalk
商铺 Shop

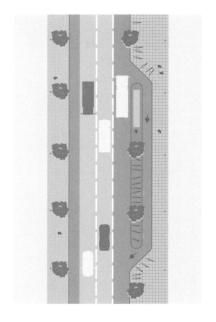

新华路平剖图–改造后
Xinhua Road plan and section after

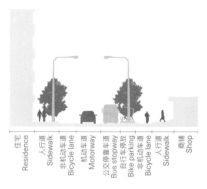

住宅 Residence
人行道 Sidewalk
非机动车道 Bicycle lane
机动车道 Motorway
公交停靠车道 Bus stopway
自行车停放 Bike parking
非机动车道 Bicycle lane
人行道 Sidewalk
商铺 Shop

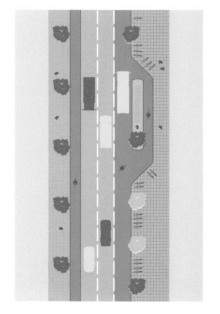

设计愿景

新华路轴测图
Xinhua Road axonometric

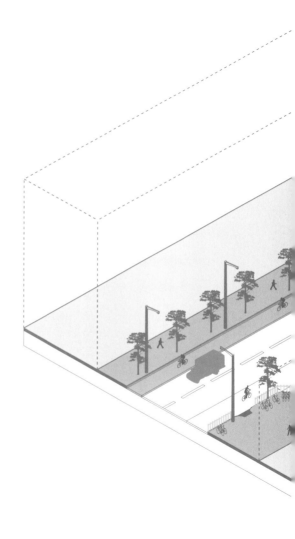

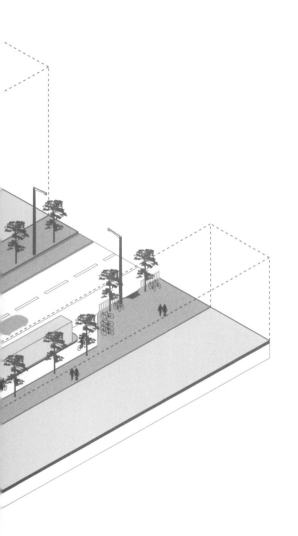

Lanxi Road and North Meiling Road

Lanxi Road has a small intersection of two crossing two-lane roads, carrying small volume of motor vehicles. It has three main problems, firstly there's no separation between the bicycles lanes and motorways, and no protection on the cyclists; second, the waiting zone for cyclists is not reasonably planned, where the cyclists will easily block the passengers when standing on the zebra crossing and the cyclists turning right from behind (see "Lanxi Road plan before", p. 286).

This design takes inspirations from the Dutch streets and intersections to separate the cycling area from the motor lanes. We also introduced isolation zone at the corner to protect the cyclists as well as to move forward the cyclists' waiting zone before the zebra stripes, which will help to avoid blocking the passengers while making enough space to the cyclists turning right from behind (see "Lanxi Road axonometric", p. 287).

兰溪路梅岭北路

该路口为双车道交叉的小路口，来往的机动车辆较少。此路口的问题，主要有两点：一为机非不隔离，骑行者不受保护；二为等候区设置不合理，骑行者等候红灯时不但占用了斑马线，阻滞了过往的行人，也容易挡住后方右转骑行流线（见"兰溪路平剖图–改造前"，P286）。

我们在设计上参考了荷兰道路路口的设计，首先进行了机非隔离，并在转角处引入隔离岛以保护骑行者；其次将骑行等候区提至斑马线前。这样的处理不但能避免挡住过马路的人流，还能让出道路空间给后方右转的骑行者（见"兰溪路轴测图"，P287）。

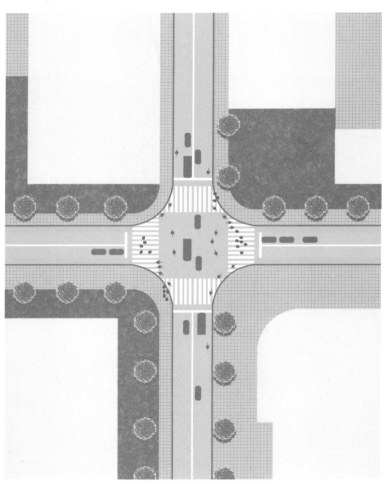

兰溪路平面图–改造后
Lanxi Road plan after

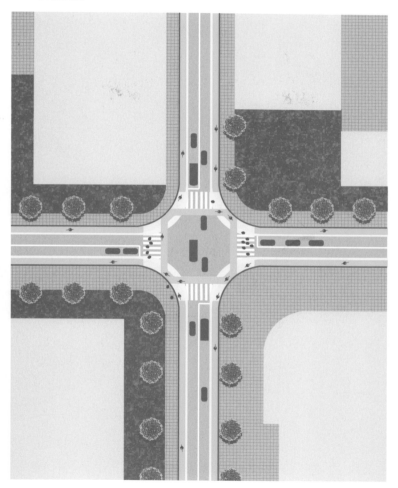

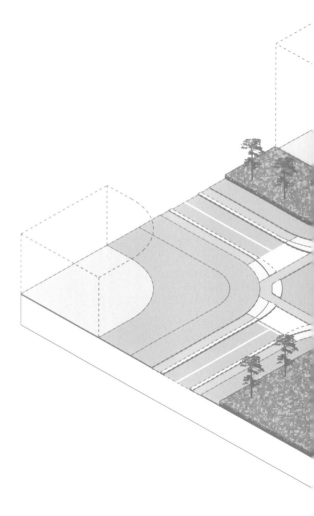

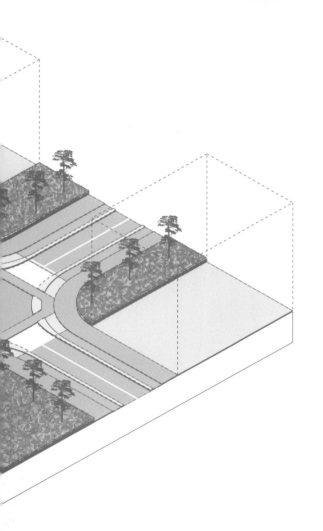

Shiguang Road Metro Sation

Shiguang Road Metro Station is located on Zhongyuan Road. There is a small area for bicycle parking near the entrance, and there is a bicycle parking strip on the sidewalk. As the terminal of Line 8, residents living in the north and larger east region of the station all flock into this station. Although a parking area is planned along the road at the entrance No. 1, the area is occupying the sidewalk space, and will cause inconvenience to pedestrians. Besides, there are a huge number of bicycles, and some of them have to be parked far from the metro station, which formed a long belt of bicycles that is over 100 meters, especially in the northeast side of the metro station (see "Shiguang Road Metro Station plan and section before", p. 294).

We suggest building a vertical bicycle parking station over the No. 1 exit. It will not only increase the parking capacity of the metro station, but also allow cyclists to directly get into the metro station after parking. Meanwhile, the one way bicycle lane on Zhongyuan Rd will be changed into two ways, which will provide the cyclists with easier access to the parking facility (see "Shiguang Road Metro Station axonometric", pp. 296 – 297).

市光路地铁站

市光路地铁站位于中原路上，为轨道交通8号线的终点站。地铁出入口附近有小型块状自行车停放区，人行道上有自行车停车带。因市光路为地铁8号线的终点站，故该站以北及以东大片区域的居民出行均需在此乘坐地铁。虽然目前本站1号口已规划了路侧停车，但这一规划挤压了人行道空间，给往来行人带来不便。此外，由于自行车数量众多，部分自行车不得不停放在离地铁口较远的区域，绵延近百米，以该站东北角最为严重（见"市光路地铁站平剖图–改造前"，P294）。

我们建议取消路侧停车，将人行道还给行人，改在1号口上建造立体自行车停车站，以增加地铁口附近的自行车停放能力，并方便骑行者停完车后直接进入地铁口。同时，将中原路的单向非机动车道改为双向，让骑行者更容易抵达立体停车设施（见"市光路地铁站轴测图"，P296–P297）。

市光路地铁站平剖图–改造前
Shiguang Road Metro Station plan and section before

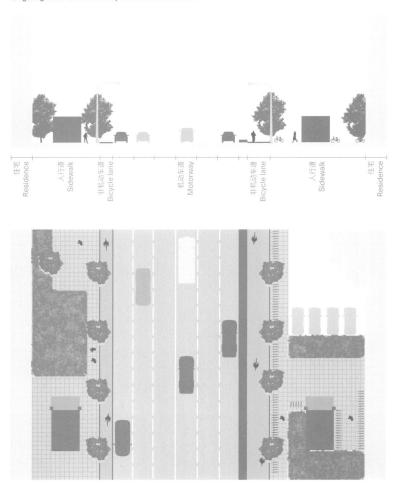

住宅 Residence　人行道 Sidewalk　非机动车道 Bicycle lane　机动车道 Motorway　非机动车道 Bicycle lane　人行道 Sidewalk　住宅 Residence

市光路地铁站平剖图–改造后
Shiguang Road Metro Station plan and section after

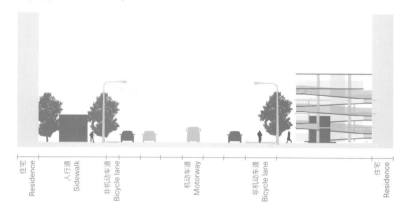

住宅
Residence

人行道
Sidewalk

非机动车道
Bicycle lane

机动车道
Motorway

非机动车道
Bicycle lane

住宅
Residence

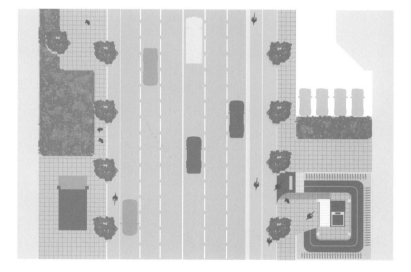

市光路地铁站轴测图
Shiguang Road Metro Station axonometric

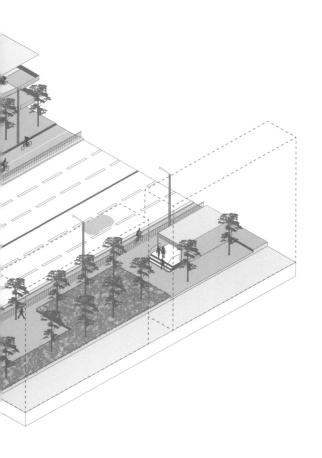

Jiangning Road (Close to Haifang Road)

Jiangning Road is north-south bound and is an important road in Jing'an District. It has 4 lanes, and each side of the road is set up with an independent cycle lane, which was isolated from the motorway with a green belt. Since the bus station is set on the isolation zone, every time when the bus enters the station, lots of people will walk across between the sidewalk and the isolation zone, which not only break the continuity of cycling, but also brings safety problems to the pedestrians (see "Jiangning Road plan and section before", p. 302).

The design suggested moving the isolation zone to the middle of the motorway to form a bus lane. Also the zone will be extend to the intersection, so the pedestrians will be able walk to the intersection and then cross the road guided by the traffic light. This design helps to organize the fragmented flows, and to avoid the conflict between pedestrians and cyclists, and will further bring a more continuous cycling experience to the cyclists (see "Jiangning Road axonometric", pp. 304−305).

江宁路(近海防路)

该路段南北走向，是静安区一条重要道路。本路段为4车道，在道路两侧设有单独的非机动车道，与机动车道之间有绿化隔离带。由于沿路的公交站台设在机非隔离岛上，每到公交车进站时间，会有批量的行人在人行道和隔离岛之间穿行，行人数量多且分散，不但打断了骑行车流，同时也造成安全隐患(见"江宁路平剖图-改造前"，P302)。

我们将原来的公交站台移至机动车道中间，形成公交车专用车道。同时将该站台移至路口处，上下公交车的行人在隔离岛上行走即可抵达路口，在路口处再根据红绿灯过马路。这样的设计规整了原本较为零散的人流，避免了乘客与骑行者的流线冲突，同时可给骑行者带来了较为流畅的骑行体验（见"江宁路轴测图"，P304-P305）。

江宁路平剖图-改造前
Jiangning Road plan and section before

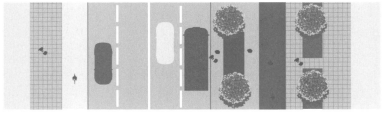

商业
Business

人行道
Sidewalk

非机动车道
Bicycle lane

机动车道
Motorway

公交车站
Bus station

非机动车道
Bicycle lane

人行道
Sidewalk

办公楼
Office

江宁路平剖图–改造后
Jiangning Road plan and section after

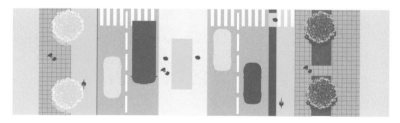

商业
Business

人行道
Sidewalk

非机动车道
Bicycle lane

机动车道
Motorway

公交车站
Bus station

机动车道
Motorway

非机动车道
Bicycle lane

人行道
Sidewalk

办公楼
Office

设计愿景

303

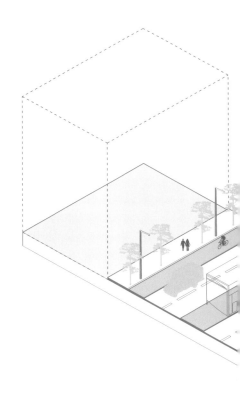

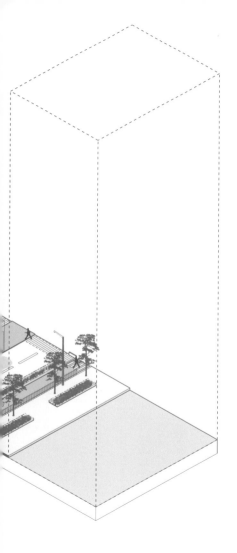

Changning Road

It is the main road in Changning District and has six motorways, two cycle lanes and sidewalks. At the east section of West Zhongshan Road rests the Zhongshan Park Commercial Street and Caojiadu Commercial Street. Since the surroundings is business area with deficient of parking spaces along the roads, many drivers would park their motor vehicles in non-motor vehicle lanes to get easier access to the shopping malls, which has blocked the cycling lane. Such situation forces the cyclists change their path to the motorway, which further threatened the cyclists' personal safety (see "Changning Road plan and section before", p. 310).

The design narrowed the width of part of the sidewalk and added temporary parking spaces along the road. A buffer zone of 60 cm is designed between the cycle lane and parking area. The two sides of the cycle lane will be slightly elevated to clarify the boundaries and to prevent motor vehicles driving across the border (see Changning Road axonometric, pp. 312 – 313).

长宁路

此条道路为长宁区的主干道路，全线双向共6条机动车道、2条非机动车道及人行道。中山西路以东一带为繁华的中山公园商业街以及曹家渡商业街。由于周边是繁华的商业区，并且路边缺少停车位，不少机动车为方便购物直接将车停泊于非机动车道上，阻挡了骑行流线，造成骑行者被迫变道至机动车道，并进一步造成安全隐患（见"长宁路平剖图–改造前"，P310）。

我们减少了部分人行道宽度，并在临近店铺门口处增设临时停车位，以供机动车泊车。而在停车位与自行车道之间设计了60 cm宽隔离带，作为下车时的缓冲带。道路两侧自行车道会略为抬高，以明确机非各自界限，防止机动车越界（见"长宁路轴测图"，P312–P313）。

长宁路平剖图–改造前
Changning Road plan and section before

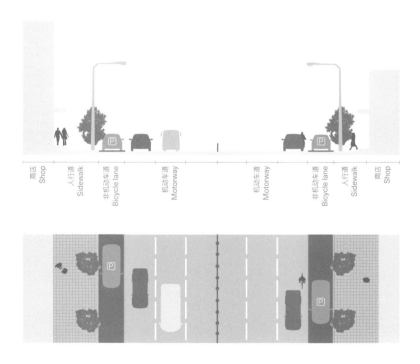

商店
Shop

人行道
Sidewalk

非机动车道
Bicycle lane

机动车道
Motorway

机动车道
Motorway

非机动车道
Bicycle lane

人行道
Sidewalk

商店
Shop

长宁路平剖图–改造后
Changning Road plan and section after

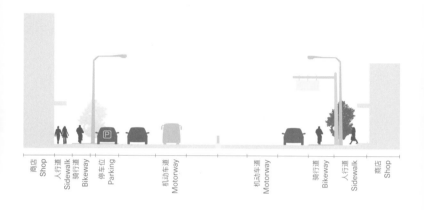

商店 Shop
人行道 Sidewalk
骑行道 Bikeway
停车位 Parking
机动车道 Motorway
机动车道 Motorway
骑行道 Bikeway
人行道 Sidewalk
商店 Shop

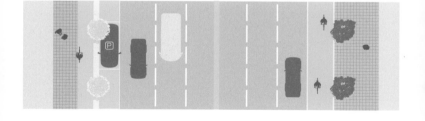

长宁路轴测图
Changning Road axonometric

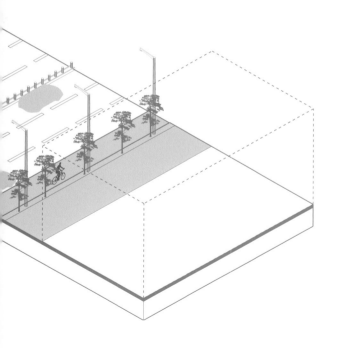

图片来源 Image sources and credits:

P24 – P25: https://kknews.cc/zh-my/history/
qnmar3y.html; P42 – P43: https://www.weibo.com/
ttarticle/p/show?id=23093510004439822513009
44097; P96 – P97: http://www.fyggzxc.com/article.
asp?Action=View&ArticleID=667&Catalog=2;
P104 – P105: 版权：阿特·克莱/荷兰摄影博物馆
Aart Klein/Nederlands Fotomuseum, https://
architectenweb.nl/nieuws/artikel.aspx?ID=40258;
P112 – P113: 版权：唐湘漪©Xiangyi Tang

课程支持：上海交通大学建筑系四年级
"先锋建筑师设计工作室"
第一轮研究团队：付炜杰，李佳雯，施捷雨，魏宇琦，
徐旖旎，周诗耀，张天韵
第二轮研究团队：陈柱燊，黄涛，刘梦迪，金池，
金梦怡，寿成彬，唐慧莲，殷正，张愉源，朱奕臣
图纸绘制：吴龙，余若琦，李思乐
撰文：王卓尔
翻译：许嘉，Marlon Zenden, Edward Tse
摄影：唐湘漪，王卓尔

Course Support: 4th Grade, Department of
Architecture Shanghai Jiao Tong University
"Advanced Architecture Design Studio"
Research Team (round 1): Weijie Fu, Jiawen Li, Jieyu
Shi, Yuqi Wei, Yini Xu, Shiyao Zhou, Tianyun Zhang
Research team (round 2): Zhushen Chen, Tao Huang,
Mengdi Liu, Chi Jin, Mengyi Jin, Chenbin Shou,
Huilian Tang, Zheng Yin, Yuyuan Zhang, Yichen Zhu
Drawing Team: Long Wu, Ruoqi Yu, Sile Li
Text: Zhuo'er Wang
Translation: Xu Jia, Marlon Zenden, Edward Tse
Photography: Xiangyi Tang, Zhuo'er Wang

本书得以面世需感谢以下两者资助
The book is made possible through financial support
from following two sponsors:

风行折叠车品牌
fnhon folding Bicycle

"北京未来城市设计高精尖创新中心——城市设计理论方
法体系研究"，项目编号UDC2016010100
Urban Design Theory and Method Research Group,
Bejing Advanced Innovation Center for Future Urban
Design: UDC2016010100

图书在版编目(CIP)数据

骑行上海：关于骑行规划的思考：汉、英 /
王卓尔著. — 上海：同济大学出版社, 2019.3
　　ISBN 978-7-5608-8198-0

　　Ⅰ. ①骑... Ⅱ. ①王... Ⅲ. ①自行车－公共交通系统
－研究－上海－汉、英 Ⅳ. ①U491.2

中国版本图书馆CIP数据核字(2018)第237237号

骑行上海：关于骑行规划的思考
Cycling@Shanghai:
A Guide to Cycle Infrastructure
王卓尔 著
Zhuo'er Wang

出品人：华春荣
责任编辑：袁佳麟　李争
装帧设计：Haller Brun (Amsterdam)
设计辅助：吴龙
责任校对：徐春莲
出版发行：同济大学出版社
上海市杨浦区四平路1239号 邮政编码：200092
http://www.tongjipress.com.cn
经销：全国各地新华书店
版次：2019年3月第1版
印次：2019年3月第1次印刷
印刷：上海雅昌艺术印刷有限公司
开本：787 mm × 1092 mm 1/36
印张：8.5 插页 5
字数：214 000
书号：ISBN 978-7-5608-8198-0
定价：128.00 元

Publisher: Chunrong Hua
Executive Editor: Crisie Yuan, Zheng Li
Book Design: Haller Brun (Amsterdam)
Design Coordination: Long Wu

National Library of China Cataloguing-in-
Publication Data. A catalogue record for this book
is available from the National Library of China
ISBN 978-7-5608-8198-0

Tongji University Press books may be purchased
at special quantity discounts for business or sales
promotional use. For information, please visit:
http://www.tongjipress.com.cn

Printed and Bound in the People's Republic of China.

Luminocity.cn

光 明 城

LUMINOCITY

光明城是同济大学出版社城市、建筑、设计专业出版品牌，成立于2012年，由群岛工作室负责策划及出版，致力以更新的出版理念、更敏锐的视角、更积极的态度，回应今天中国城市、建筑、设计领域的问题。LUMINOCITY, a high-end professional publishing brand specialized in urbanism & architecture, was founded in 2012 as a subsidiary of Tongji University Press. The brand, run by Studio Archipelago and based in Beijing and Shanghai, is responsible for the entire production of works and distinguishes itself by high quality and specialty.